Pigeon Hill

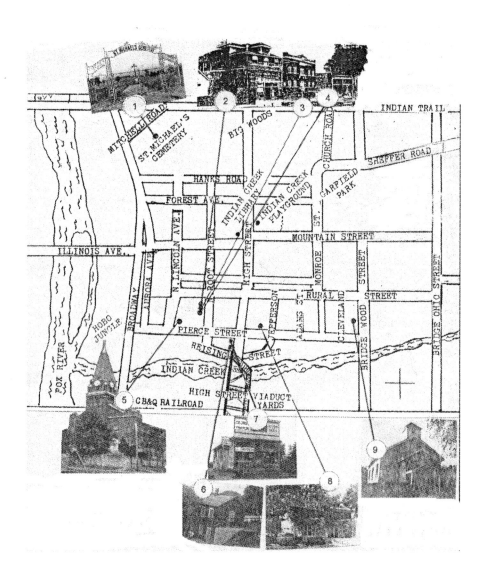

ROMANIAN COMMUNITY
1. St. Michael's Cemetery; 2. Olar Drug Store; 3. Casa Romana Hall; 4. Frunzar Grocery Store; 5. St. Michael's Church; 6. Duplex, Reising Street; 7. Trippon Grocery Store; 8. Fiji Grocery Store; 9. Romanian Baptist Church

PIGEON HILL

▼

Growing Up Romanian and Mom's Story

Short Stories of the Life and Times
1908–1932
In Aurora Illinois

George W. Trippon and Mary Trippon

Writers Club Press
San Jose New York Lincoln Shanghai

Pigeon Hill
Growing Up Romanian and Mom's Story

All Rights Reserved © 2001 by George W. Trippon

No part of this book may be reproduced or transmitted in any form or by any means, graphic, electronic, or mechanical, including photocopying, recording, taping, or by any information storage retrieval system, without the permission in writing from the publisher.

Writers Club Press
an imprint of iUniverse, Inc.

For information address:
iUniverse, Inc.
5220 S. 16th St., Suite 200
Lincoln, NE 68512
www.iuniverse.com

ISBN: 0-595-20899-1

Printed in the United States of America

CONTENTS

LIST OF ILLUSTRATIONS vii
Preface ix
Acknowledgments xi
Prologue xiii

Growing Up Romanian
    Church 1
    Romanian Church 3
    Holidays–Christmas and Pigs 5
    Pigs and the Holidays 7
    Holidays–Easter 8
    The Fourth of July 11
    Here Come the Brides 12
    The Trippon Grocery Store 15
    Store and Living Quarters 19
    Store Basement 22
    Gas Station 24
    Big Theater Barn 27
    World War One 29
    Medicines 31
    Medicine Shows 34
    Gypsies/Pigeon Hill 36
    Superstitions-Mail Orders 38
    The Hobo Jungle 42
    Election Day and the Grocery Store 44
    Bootlegging and Whiskey 45

Murder *47*
Leg Accident *49*
Boy Scouts *51*
Sport Times and Sad Times *53*

Mom's Story
Coming to America *92*
Yanco Stirs the Fire *99*
Dan's Disobedience Brought Me Luck *101*
So Different and So New! *107*
A Home and Reverses *122*
Return of the Native *139*
California, The Golden *152*

Epilogue 155
About the Author 157

LIST OF ILLUSTRATIONS

Romanian church funerals–two photos 55
Romanian church funerals–two photos 55
Romanian Christmas & the Vitfliam 58
Home funeral 59
Casa Romana Hall 59
Mom–18 years old 60
Mom & Pop's wedding day 61
Mom & Pop's wedding party 62
John Silagyi's wedding 63
George Pop's wedding 64
Emma & Victor Trense's wedding day–two photos 65
Trippon Grocery Store exterior–two photos 66
Grocery store interior–two photos 67
Grocery store interior 68
Credit sales slips 1920's 69
Gas station and garage–two photos 71
Reising Street house–two photos 71
CB&Q locomotive 73
The roundhouse 73
Pop's family–four photos 74
Babies Marika & George–three photos 78

Trippon children–four photos 79
Trippon children–three photos 80
Teenage Mary Ann & George 86
Mom's passport 87
Maria & Rosie 90
George's charcoal portrait 52
Mom's 95th birthday 91

Preface

This series of short stories about Pigeon Hill, Aurora, Illinois was encouraged in order to record a personal history of the Romanian Community from 1908 to the early 1930's. The first part of this book details my memories of a beautiful childhood.

My mother started to tell her life story in 1951. The story telling was recorded as she told short versions of the stages of life in Romania, the voyage to America, her life in Ohio, and finally to her marriage in Aurora, Illinois and Pigeon Hill.

I've heard my mother's stories many times. I've included Mom's story from the time of her departure from Romania to the early years in America on Pigeon Hill.

The many early photographs of the church funerals show the congregations of the day. The weddings are a delight for the fashions of that period. Photos include family, relatives, the grocery store and many other early memories. Many of the photos are in the archives of the Aurora Historical Museum.

Acknowledgments

I am deeply indebted to Jo and Dan Trippon for their generous assistance and cooperation for their time and patience in the preparation of this book.

I am also indebted to many people who answered many questions about the early years of the 20's and 30's. A gracious thank you to Russell Onak, Emma (Oros) Bonye, Leona (Boyne) Banks, Annie (Kuk) Waisvillas, and to childhood friends throughout our lives; the late John Terebesy and Alex Demeter.

A special thank you to Leon Ardelean for his assistance on the history of St. Michael's Church and his recent photos of locals on Pigeon Hill.

To the memory of my dear friend and cousin, Lucille Trippon for our early years. The many discussions about the church and the many customs we embraced. Some of the memorabilia we exchanged is now in the archives of the Aurora Historical Museum. My thanks to the Executive Director John R. Jaros; Curator, Dennis Buck; and Jackie Shanahan for all their assistance.

I am indebted to Bill Becker and to Lynda Becker who assisted in the preparation of the typescript, their reading and corrections of the manuscript and the skillful scanning of Mom's collection of old photographs. I am grateful for their support and personal kindness.

My greatest thanks to James W. Price for his encouragement and for his support for the many years while working on this book.

Prologue

The American Indian was displaced from his lands and the lands were replaced with the displaced peoples of many lands.

Aurora, Illinois was the first city in the world to have lights electrically light up the streets. The name "Aurora" is so named to honor a local Indian chief. His name was Waubonsie, which means "Morning Light."

The present city site was part of the Pottawatomie Indian village situated on the Fox River. The river divided the downtown area from the prairies that spread beyond the confines and through the northern state. This gave Illinois the name of Prairie State. The area of Pigeon Hill goes north to the Big Woods, east to Indian Creek just past Farnsworth Avenue, south to the railroad yards and West to the Fox River.

The Potawatomi Indians were a tribe of the Great Algonquin tribes. Their tribes stretched from the Atlantic to the Mississippi and westward.

Between the wars with the Ottawa, Chippewa and Iroquois tribes and the English invaders, the Potawatomi tribe fought the great battle against the Illinois tribe with the help of the Kickapoo tribe. The battle took place near LaSalle Illinois at the large rock on the Illinois River. This rock rose 100 feet or more above the Illinois River. The top of the rock measured over an acre. A treacherous path leads the only way to the top. The Illinois tribe took refuge here. They were starved to death. A few survived. Today it is called Starved Rock. The Potawatomi tribe settled into the prairies of northern Illinois and parts of western Indiana.

This branch of the tribe was known as the Prairie Potawatomi (they settled along the Illinois River and its tributary, the Mississippi). The tribe settled west of Chicago along the Fox River, which flowed southwesterly into the Illinois River.

To the northeast end of town, some half-dozen blocks east of the river, grew the community known as Pigeon Hill. Here, at the turn of the century, in the early nineteen hundreds, came the many settlers from many countries. The principal settlers were the peoples from Luxembourg, the peoples from Romania, the peoples from Hungary and later the Mexican Nationals...in that order.

To the south of Pigeon Hill was the High Street viaduct, which spanned across the Indian Creek, the Burlington C.B.&Q. Railroad and railroad yards. The viaduct linked the overspill of the Romanian and Luxembourg colonies, one to the other.

To the north of the hill were the big woods. The big woods stretched from northeast of downtown Aurora; from the banks of the Fox River, past Garfield Park to the farmlands of the east.

So, Pigeon Hill!

This story is about the Romanian heritage on Pigeon Hill in Aurora, Illinois circa 1908 through 1932.

Growing Up Romanian

Church

Life for the Romanian population revolved around the church. In the early 1900's there was no Romanian church. The Luxemburg (German) population had the St. Joseph Roman Catholic Church on North High Street. The first masses in the Romanian Tongue were held in St. Joseph's Auditorium. The Romanian students also attended class with the Luxemburg students. The classes (1920 to 1924) included learning reading, writing and language. Classes included prayers in German and in English, arithmetic and music. The violin was the popular instrument of the day. Piano and voice lessons graced all the students.

My oldest sister Emma learned the violin. She won the violin contest, but she was disqualified because she was not a member of St. Joseph Church. Emma never played the violin again. Emma also won the spelling bee but was denied the prize. Emma questioned why. She did the wrong thing to question. For this she had to roll down her stockings below her knees. With her bare knees she had to kneel in this square box filled with raw kernels of corn. She then had to pray six Hail Marys kneeling with a straight rigid back posture. The boys rolled down their stockings for the same punishment. Actually, the German students, the nuns and the priest were mean to the Romanian students. The Romanian students were disliked and detested. There were a few sympathetic German students who did engage in friendships.

The punishments, not confined just to the Romanian students, were really corporal. Girls and boys alike suffered the kneeling in the corn kernels as they recited (silently) the required punishment of prayers. The priest was sadistic. He pulled one's ears—the upper ears pulled to almost lift you from the floor. The lower ear always seemed more sensitive. The coup de grace was the baton. You held your hands cupped into the air. Your thumb, forefinger and middle finger pinched together, the tips of the three all lined up evenly. These three digits held up in the air. The priest now lifts the baton. He switches it up in the air. He aims the tip and snapping it down sharply and quickly upon the three fingers and he jerks the switch back up and down in a rhythm—a whip, a lash, quickly until you see the red welts and you feel the stings. For fear of embarrassment no one being punished ever cried. Tears, yes. Voices, never. The ultimate punishment was being locked in the basement during lunch hour. This happened at St. Michael's School. We had our ears pulled here too. We also knelt in corn kernels. We were actually slapped across the face. Punishment for what? Tardiness, whispering in class, falling out of line (all classes always lined up to march out of classes in an orderly manner), pushing, giggling in class, ad nauseam.

Freedom came when we all started to go to public schools. So Brady School—here come the Romanians.

Romanian Church

The First Romanian Church was built in 1908 and dedicated in 1909. The St. Michael's Romanian Greek Catholic Church sits at the corner of Lincoln Avenue and Pierce Street. It sat back from the corner next to the alley. The Church became the school. The New Church built in about 1916 sits on the actual corner of Pierce and Lincoln Avenues.

The Bell Tower is adorned on four sides of the steeple with large clocks. The clock always tolled when a parishioner died. We all knew who had died. We all knew who had been ill. The entire membership of the church attended the funeral mass and almost all walked behind the deceased as the cortege marched up Pierce Street, left on High Street to Mountain Street, down to St. Michael's cemetery on North Broadway. Pierce Street was still an unpaved street in the early 1920's. When Pierce Street was finally paved with tar, the kids enjoyed digging and chewing the soft black tar. We always dug deep for clean tar when the hot weather came, and we chewed.

The children loved the memorial (wake) prayer meetings. The meetings took place at the home of the family of the deceased. For each child there was a home baked cupcake with a nickel embedded atop the center. This was given in memory of the deceased. I personally attended every funeral during my childhood. The adults fared much better. Across their cupcake was an accordion pleated dollar bill arched across as a handle, pinned at each end to the cupcake. This to be enjoyed for a drink in memory of the deceased. We all made our wine then. We also had a homemade beer, called near beer (eek).

You will notice the many beautiful photos of the funerals. The custom was to photograph the deceased with all the loved relatives and the parishioners surrounding the open coffin. Notice the clocks. The clocks strike the hour and the half hour 24 hours a day to this day. The bell ringer pulled the thick rope that hung down low from the belfry above. The rope had a couple of large knots near the ends. The rope was located in back of the church behind the pews of the balcony. He'd pull the rope almost to the floor. BONG! Then the rope would fly up and the bell ringer would fly up too, as he grasped the rope. Up, down …Sometimes we would be allowed to hang on too. Up and down. Ahh, I loved that balcony.

    I remember the grocery store. I started working there as a child. I loved it and hated it. The Indian Creek and the Fox River gave me my happiest hours. The Indian Creek runs into Aurora's east side, from the northeast end of Pigeon Hill, flows down over the dam (under the High Street viaduct) and empties into the Fox River just south of Pierce Street. Pigeon Hill was part of the Fox River Valley. I recall having two homing pigeons when I was about 8 years old. History has it that there were many pigeons on the Hill area. So–Pigeon Hill!

Holidays–Christmas and Pigs

The Romanian Christmas was celebrated a week after the customary Roman Catholic Church's Holy Day. The Romanian Easter followed the Western Easter Orthodox Calendar, the Old Julian Calendar. The new Gregorian calendar is the Calendar we have in use now.

    The church choir and some of the parishioners donned military type costumes, and we called them the Vitfliam. Each represented a character in a play that was presented in each and every parishioner's home. The play portrayed the Three Wise Men on their way to Bethlehem. Besides the soldiers there was King Herod. He was on his way to conduct the census count. Two shepherds also accompanied the group. They had all seen the Bright Star of Bethlehem. The play lasted fifteen minutes plus. Please note the photograph of the Church elders and the Vitfliam in costumes. We all loved the headpieces, High Crowns beautifully covered in bright satins with jewels and ropes of glittering silver and gold ropes of tinsel. Note the staffs of the shepherds. The staffs have Jingle Bells wrapped around the poles. The shepherds pounded the poles at each home to announce their arrival. The Vitfliam visited over a hundred homes each holiday season. This was an exciting time for all ages. Groups of children went door to door and sang Christmas carols according to their age groups. We all carried our homemade sacks (bags) with handles. We received candies, walnuts, mixed nuts, homemade Romanian baked breads, sweets (Kifla) and apples and oranges.

    I recall one Christmas I joined a group of smaller children (my age group). I was tall and skinny. The song our group sang was the most basic simple song for a child to sing. We sang our little hearts out-about a little lamb-a lost little lamb-who was found. The lyrics sang out "Where were you little lamb?" At one home the lady said to me that I should be ashamed to sing such simple carols. I should learn the bigger songs. I never caroled again. At church, though, I sang my little heart out. There were actually two Sunday morning Masses. At Christmas everyone came to the High Mass.

In the living room Pop always placed the tall Christmas tree in front of the back window. We all helped with the decorations. The silver, glittering garlands draped near the ends of each branch. Carefully the candleholders were clipped at the end of each branch. Candles were arranged by color, the reds, the greens and the whites. The shimmering baubles graduated in size from the larger at the bottom of the Christmas tree to the smaller sizes near the top. The silver star was at the very top.

The candles were lighted just before the Vitfliam arrived for their skit. This was Christmas Eve. There was wine on the table and all the goodies of Christmas: rolls and sweets made from poppy seed, raisins and walnuts, prune jelly, and cinnamon sugar.

After the group left the gifts were passed around.

Christmas Day, the candles were lighted at breakfast, at lunch, and at dinner. They were also lighted each time a new customer arrived to see our tree.

The gifts I received from Mom and Pop were enjoyed by all of us. For a few days. My beautiful huge white rocking horse was sold the third day after Christmas. The three plaid shirts, one red, one green, and one navy plaid were my Cowboy shirts. Mom sold two of them to Alex and Justin's mom. After I no longer rode my bicycle to grade school, the bike was sold. I was too busy to miss any of the gifts.

Pigs and the Holidays

Indian summer was a welcome relief after the hot days and the rains and lightning of the summer.

The many Romanian families now planned the events of the coming holidays. First on any list was the butchering of a pig. I always accompanied my pop to the particular farm out beyond the big woods. There were many large pigs. There was also a smell in the air. Pop and the farmer checked out the pig we wanted. It was exciting to watch the farmer jump the fence and take off for the proposed pig. The farmer lassoed the pig with a rope—a la Tom Mix. He dragged the squealing, fighting pig into the yard. He closed the gate behind him. A straw fire was burning in a pit. There were also live coals. Sitting in the fire was a red-hot long poker. The farmer picked up the cold end of the poker. He plunged the red-hot tip into the side of the pig's head just below the ear. The pig grunted as he rolled over and up with his legs in the air. The pig was laid upon the burning straw. You could smell the charred hair and skin.

We all had a taste of the pig's ears and the tail. These were cut off as a treat to all the family. At home, in the basement, the butchering began. Every part of the pig became a meal. Pig's feet jellied with paprika, pork chops, roasts, and bacon. The intestines were carefully removed and washed clean, inside and outside. These became the casings for the famous garlic sausage. Today one can purchase casings (in salt) in many ethnic grocery stores. The other sausage was blood sausage. The liver became my favorite liver sausage.

My pop was famous for his garlic sausage. It became a staple in sales in the grocery store. We made yards and yards of it. The machine we used is now on display at the Aurora Historical Museum in Aurora Illinois.

Holidays–Easter

We loved Easter Sunday. The Easter basket parade started early. Some parishioners crossed over the High Street Bridge from their homes in that area. Others came from the eastern area of Pigeon Hill down High Street, others down Reising Street, and down High Street and to Pierce Street, south to Lincoln Avenue. The sight outside the church was awesome. Some families carried large laundry type baskets. Others carried smaller baskets. Baskets were each covered with beautiful hand embroidered tablecloths or decorated homespun towels. Inside the baskets were the Easter dinners: baked hams, roasted chickens, garlic sausages, homemade breads and nut and raisin-filled sweets. Apples and oranges and candies completed the foods.

The church basement was decorated in Easter colors. The parishioners displayed their individual baskets in row after row in aisle after aisle. The blessing ceremony of the baskets would take place after the High Mass services.

After Mass, the families would stand behind their Easter Basket. The Priest and the Altar Boys would walk slowly up and down each aisle. The Altar Boys carried a large vessel of Holy Water in front of the Priest. The Priest carried a bouquet of rosemary branches tied together with a yellow ribbon. He also carried a small cross in his hand. As the prayers were spoken, the Priest would dip the branches into the Holy Water. As he walked slowly he splashed the Holy Water over the baskets and over the families. Of course, some of the kids walked up and down the aisle in concert with the Priest. They were really blessed and wet. The High Mass of the Easter Services contains the most beautiful music and words

A cappella. The parishioner's voices blended so beautifully with the lead cantors

After the blessings we all took out our colored Easter eggs. We played a game. We challenged each other with the striking of the eggs. We cupped an egg in one hand and the challenger held his egg cupped so as to hit the egg. We called this head to head. If the striker smacked and broke the egg, you lost the egg. If your egg did not break, you turned your egg and the challenger did the same and you hit his egg. As the game progressed we would peel the egg and we would eat it.

I remember the very young years, my folks would fill a basin with warm water. Mom would place two colored Easter eggs and a coin in the water. The first child to awaken and wash his hands in that water would receive both the lucky eggs and the coin. The coin I still have is a $5.00 gold piece.

The Romanian Baptist Church opened on Wood Street in the late 20's. On Saturday mornings I loved to watch and listen to the group. The group had a prayer meeting in public across the street from our store. The tambourines fascinated me as they rattled and beat the rhythms to beautiful hymns. I had to have a tambourine. After all, Valentino was here. The gaucho costume was in (ah, the bloomers became Spanish). A new scenario was born. We did the tango, we beat the tambourine and we ate my favorite candy bar, the Tango.

Easter time was also the fashion time for new suits for guys and fancy hats and dresses for gals. The early 20's still showed long dresses. 1926 brought out the flapper age. Long hair was cut off. Bangs were in. Spit curls were in. Dresses came above the knee. Silk stockings were rolled below the knee. Long beads were in. Smoking became the rage for women. Long cigarette holders and lighters became the vogue.

My mother cut her hip length hair into a "bob". She had a marcelled wave. That was the time my money disappeared and she went to Romania and Europe. We all dressed in our Easter best. New dresses for the girls and ladies. New suits for the boys and the men. My mom and several lady relatives, each with their sons in tow, took the third rail to Chicago. We're off to a shopping spree. A special bus drove us to Maxwell Street. The streets were open every weekend. Several blocks were converted with stalls and card tables filled with dry goods, blankets, bedding, toys, tools, dresses, work clothes and fruit stands. Many of the stores had special sales. We found the suit store. Mrs. Julia and her son, John and my mom and I picked out our suits, tried them on, approved them, and the suits were paid for and wrapped. "Hold on to your suit, under your arm and hold on tight. You don't want someone to grab it!" We held on. We bought shoes with laces. I was happy because I had a time with the button hook when I tried to button seven buttons on each shoe We shopped for the new underwear called BVD's–one piece sleeveless underwear with short legs (above the knee), and with a drop seat with two side buttons, in light weight cotton, with a button down front. We met many other Romanian families shopping, girls with packages and new ribbons in their hair. We were now all ready for Easter. I was 10 years old.

The Fourth of July

The most exciting holiday was the celebration of the Fourth of July.

The front window displayed all kinds of fireworks. Ladyfingers (rows and rows of tiny firecrackers), one-inch salutes, two-inch salutes, sparklers, roman candles, snakes (A pyramid brown shape of incense. You lighted the tip with a match and a thick ribbon of brown thick ash substance crawled circling around.), rockets large and small, and lantern shaped balloons. These balloons were made of a crepe paper texture in striped red and white colors. The bottom had a wooden ring. Nestled in the center of the ring were the crisscrossed wires that held the metal cup with the special liquid. Grown-ups gathered in the streets to help and to watch. One would stretch the balloon to its full length and extend the sides by hand. Someone else would light the liquid in the cup and we waited. Slowly the balloon started to inflate. Soon the balloon moved slightly. When fully filled, the balloon was released. Floating slowly into the air the balloon went up and up and away. Many farms and homes caught fire from landing balloons. But each year we sold a lot of balloons.

The fireworks display was in the front window area next to the cigar/cigarette counter carefully wire screened from the public. We never suffered a mishap.

Here Come the Brides

"Romanian" weddings at St. Michael's Church were always attended by the entire parish. No one had to be "invited" to the wedding or to the festivities held at St. Michael's Hall.

The church wedding ceremony was always incorporated into the Mass service. I remember the beauty of so many wedding services in church.

In 1931 when my oldest sister was married, she had 15 bridesmaids. Every bride had all her girl relatives as bridesmaids. No one asked, it was just the way it was.

After the church services the bridal party and all the guests moved out of the church to the Casa Romana. Many people walked the one block from the church via the alley passageway to Root Street.

The banquet tables were ready, the food was ready, the guests were ready and the bride and groom were ready. Baked breads, chicken, garlic sausage, stuffed cabbage, potatoes, homemade pickles, salads, and the wedding cake. And homemade wines. After the toasts and after the meals were finished, everyone helped in moving the tables and chairs. The chairs were lined up all around and against the walls. You will enjoy Mom's story of the bride's dance.

Below the stage, a long table was set up parallel to the stage perimeter. This was the preparation for the best man and the matron of honor to begin the bride's dance. They were assisted by the bridesmaids. The male partners to the bridesmaids now formed a large circle in front of the table. The maid of honor prepared the large soup plates, one on top of the other, each with a silver dollar. In the 20's and early 30's everyone had and used silver dollars.

Now, the bride and the groom entered into the circle and danced the first dance. Then, one of the groom's ushers takes the bride away for a twirl. Each usher dances with the bride. Then, it's dances for sale. The maid of honor shakes and rattles the coin in the soup plate and shouts "Dance the bride." The men with each vie for the dance by aiming a silver dollar and using a forceful throw at the center of the dish. If the dish breaks, the dance is free. A new dish appears. The new coin joins the first coin. On and on it goes.

A line of men ready to dance with the bride is forming now. After each dancer has a twirl, the dancer pins money on the bride's veil. Singles, fives, tens, twenties, the idea is that the veil will become a sea of green.

The poor bride dances on and on. When the veil is green, or when the bride appears green, a cry is heard. At that point, the ushers surround the bride and grab her and lift her to crash through the circled crowd. This was the tradition then, to kidnap the bride. No one has ever kidnapped a bride.

The band starts. The crowd starts to dance. The fun has begun.

Meanwhile, the bride and groom, the best man, the maid of honor, and the parents of the bride and the groom are huddled in the office. They are counting the money. They are presenting personal bills for their particular expenses of the wedding. The rest of the money goes to the bride and groom.

My sister's wedding photos include one with the bridesmaid and ushers, the other with most of her friends and relatives.

A fashion note about the bridesmaid. Marcelled hair and everyone with a scarf tied around the head. Everyone had pink roses. The bride wore white roses. The groom worked for a floral hot house specializing in roses.

During the late festivities, my dad took me back to check on the store and the house. My little black and white puppy greeted us at the porch door, which was open. Pop dashed into the second bathroom. The large safe was out from the wall, ready to be moved. Nothing was taken. Pop switched all the lights on. He called the police. Pop locked up the place. He returned to the Romanian Hall. The puppy and I stayed guard. I was excited. I was leaving my 14th year. Next month I'd be 15. I'm going to have my own room. The sun porch is mine. After my leather couch that makes into a bed, I'm now to sleep in a day bed. No more going through Mom and Pop's bedroom at night to the living room to unlock the back door to the basement and pick up that chamber pot from the top step and pee. I'll have my own chamber pot! The basement is too cold in the wintertime. At least we did have a modern toilet in the basement. My entire youth was spent in this store.

Emma's wedding was more exciting for me because of an electric automobile. My drama teacher, Miss Thomas, from East Aurora High School drove to my dad's store in her electric automobile—the driver's seat was plush velveteen. A swivel handle protruded from the driver's side. This was the steering wheel. The back seat was upholstered in plush velvet—little drapes adorned the windows, drawn back with velvet straps/bands! There were two flower vases on either side of the windows, with fresh flowers.

Miss Thomas brought a couple of beautiful woven baskets, one with flowers and one with fruit. She let me drive up High Street and back. A beautiful memory. A most gifted teacher, Miss Thomas.

•

The Trippon Grocery Store

When Pop and Mom first bought the store, the address was 211 Pierce Street. When Pierce Street was surfaced with tar, the street blocks were renumbered starting at Broadway. The store address was now 425 Pierce Street. The store was on the southwest corner of High Street and Pierce Street. Pop also bought the property south of the store to Reising Street. At Reising Street there was a two-level house. The lower level faced Reising Street. The upper level entrance was on High Street facing north toward the store.

The front entrance of the grocery store was entered via four cement steps (see photo). The entrance was in the center front of the store. There were large show windows on each side of the entrance.

There was a small entrance on the side of the store facing High Street.

When you entered the store there was a wide center aisle. The various service counters lined each side of the aisle. At the end of the aisle there was a center door. This door led to the living quarters.

The counters were arranged in sections of merchandise and service. The first counter to the left was the tobacco area. The top section of the counter was filled with boxes of cigars, each box held open with a wire spring. When a customer picked out the cigar he wanted, we brought out the box and the customer picked out his cigar. Against the one wall was a slotted shelf that held the various packs of cigarettes; (Lucky Strike in the green package–the green color went to war in the in the early 1940's). Camels were the most popular. We loved the clown on the Clown pack of cigarettes, very colorful.

Hanging down from the top of the inside counter was the large round humidor. This was dipped in water a couple of times a week to keep the cigars moist and fresh.

The cigar counter was a busy place. The bottom shelves had the sports paraphernalia and the school supplies.

Tennis star Helen Wills introduced the visor cap in green celluloid, which became a fad, and we sold dozens of them. This was in 1925. The wall shelves behind the tobacco counter had the cutting machine for plug tobacco, and the many cans of various snuffs, canned tobaccos and cartons of all the cigarettes of the day. Of course, we had our comedians then too. A popular phone call asked if we had Prince Albert in a can. When we said "yes," they said, "Please let him out."

Adjoining the cigar counter was the cash register area, followed by a small aisle. The next counter was the ladies' counter. The wall shelves and the counter top and bottom were filled with sewing fabrics, sewing threads and embroidery threads, needles, children's shirts and skirts, socks, stockings (real silk) and tablecloths and towels. Plain tablecloths ready for the pattern designs to be embossed in the desired areas of the tablecloth. There were also men's shirts, coveralls and neckties.

Mom had many wide sheets of waxed paper which were pinpricked with many designs. There was a pie plate with a purple colored wax. This was heated to almost liquid. Mom wore a cotton glove as she placed the desired design over the cloth. With a square cloth, which she had dipped in the ink, she rubbed across the pricked designed areas. She also sold the necessary colors of the many new embroidery threads. There are blouses that were planned with these designs. They are in a photo in this book. They are worn by my three sisters.

The corner end to the left of the store was the fun corner. There was the ice cream parlor.

The store hours knew no time. Summer night hours lengthened because we had the ice cream parlor.

The Aurora Bottling Company had the best soda pop. My favorite was Delaware Punch, a grape flavor, um-um better. Pop bought a malted milk machine. The malted milk machine is now with the Aurora Historical Museum.

Then in the late 20's a new longer fancy soda pop arrived–Nehi! It came in many flavors. We sold more Nehi than all the others, including Coca Cola.

We made great cones and ice cream sandwiches. We froze ripe peeled bananas in which we placed a long round stick at one end. We dipped the bananas in melted chocolate syrup and refroze them. We had wooden flat sticks and we placed a thin round cardboard at one end. We placed a dipper of vanilla ice cream at that end. It was then dipped in the chocolate syrup and frozen. This ended when Eskimo Pie with a handle was introduced. The wrappers of Eskimo Pie were saved into tin foil balls.

A new popcorn machine half filled the front display window. The aroma filled the street at Pierce and High.

We opened early and we closed late. Many times the knocking at our porch door at 3 a.m. to 5 a.m. had Mom or Pop arise to wait on a customer who forgot milk or sandwich ham.

In the early 20's we didn't have electricity. We had a walk-in icebox. Every day large cakes of ice were delivered. All homes had iceboxes, so customers shopped smartly. The ice delivery wagon was always followed by children in the summer-time. When the delivery man used his tongs to carry the ice into the homes, the kids would step up to the back of the wagon and help themselves to the chipped pieces of ice.

Pop had ordered electricity for the store and the living quarters. Mom had shopped in Chicago and had purchased the lamp/filter fixtures. The living room's lamp fixture hung from the middle of the ceiling. Shaped like a wagon wheel it sported five filters and five bulb sockets. The corded chain supported a thin gas pipeline to the filters and electric wiring for the electric sockets. All was ready for the time we could switch from gas to electricity. Pop had a long pole with a candlewick at the top end. To light the gas filters required a ladder as each filter had a switch to turn. When the electric was finally turned on, Pop bought a radio.

Opposite the ice cream parlor with a large aisle was the meat section. A large display case with various cuts of meats. Behind this meat counter was the large walk-in meat refrigerator. There hung the sides of beef, pork and lamb cuts.

There was a small aisle. A counter, which was designed with small glass framed box type areas, formed a display as each framed area displayed rice, many kinds of beans (red, navy, lima, pinto, white, black, red and many more), dried fruits and herbs. On the walls behind were all the canned goods, vegetables, coffees, teas, paper goods and pastas. Also, there were dried mushrooms hanging from a hook. There was a stalk of bananas hanging from a hook. We used a sickle type knife to cut off the desired amounts of bananas needed.

The front counter was the candy counter. The shelves held many glass trays, which contained the finest assortment of chocolates and fancy candies available. The top of the counter held glass jars with special candies. The wall shelves behind the candy counter carried the cake flours, the syrups, the vanillas and various flavors for ethnic foods.

The front display area was the penny arcade of candies. Boxes displayed the jawbreakers, gumdrops, licorice sticks, and wax bottles with flavored liquids, lime, strawberry, grape and lemon. The candy bars were large. This was my domain.

The floor areas had display boxes of fresh fruits, potatoes, kegs of dried fish assortments, mops, brooms etc. We had it all. There was also a spittoon at the front corner of the cigar counter. It sat behind the door in a rubber-lined box.

Store and Living Quarters

Originally the store had the large area in the front section of the building. A larger room was in the back section. This section became our living quarters. Pop had a two-bedroom addition built on the back west section plus a porch. The door from the front store to the back room was in the center of the walls. The toilet was in the basement.

Now the design of the living area. Inside the living room, to the right of the door, the bathroom was planned and completed. The tub hugged the west wall. Above the tub was a window, which faced the open porch. The wall against the store area held a sink. A six foot wooden partition was put around the "Bathroom-Kitchen sink." The wall facing the living room had room for the gas stove. One side of the stove was against the wall that separated the store and the living quarters. The stove had four burners and a large upper and lower oven on the right side. Mom could do all her washing in the large washtubs here and boiling of bedclothes in the oval copper tub. This way she could keep her eyes on the incoming customers, and go to wait on them. The gas lighted hot water heater was another marvel, always scaring the hell out of us. A large cylindrical tank sitting atop a steel frame. The tank held the water, which continued via the pipe system. A large aluminum chimney rose to the ceiling into an outlet to the roof. This cylinder had large holes around the bottom. The hole facing the tub also had a long faucet that reached out over the front edge of the bathtub. This hole was also the area where the lighted match was placed as we turned this knob to release the gas to light up the gas plates. It was necessary to have a lighted match ready when you turned on the knob to light the gas jets. If gas was allowed to escape, the gas flames would ignite. The flames would blow out the large holes around the bottom edge of the water tank. The flames would flare out and up the sides of the tank with a whoosh! You immediately turned the knob off. After a few minutes you again tried to relight the gas jet. The "flared flames" scared the hell out of us. Against the south partition was Mom's sewing machine. The kitchen cabinet was next to it–a flour bin on one end that actually released amounts of flour. A countertop area–Beautiful glass doors to see the dishes, drawers galore, deep ones, shallow ones. We loved the sewing machine. When we were older, oh about 5 to 6, we played peek-a-boo!

A bathtub was a luxury in the 1920's. So our grocery store now had a "bathhouse" too. Mom and Pop rented out the tub for Friday and Saturday night baths. Women on Friday, men on Saturday. Mary and I, and later when Florence grew bigger, we'd climb onto the sewing machine and peek over the partition to see the bather. When Mom caught us the sewing machine found a new spot.

Mom had an assembly line system for our early Saturday night bath. After the water was drawn, Mary, Florence and I were submerged in the hot water. Mary was bathed first by Mom. Next to the tub were two chairs placed side by side. On each chair was draped a clean sheet. After Mary's bath she was placed in the first chair. The sheet was then wrapped around her. After Florence's bath, Mary was moved to the dry sheet and wrapped again. Florence was wrapped in the wet sheet. While this was going on, Mom would interrupt bathing to run into the store to help Pop and Emma wait on customers. Pop was the butcher. In the meantime Emma came to dress Mary and Florence. I was still soaking this particular Saturday night. I was in the tub alone. I heard Mom and the ladies laughing. I stepped out of the tub and quietly tiptoed to the door leading into the store. Mom was on the other side of the counter at the scale. A live chicken, wings folded, was lying on the scale. Three or four women were looking up at the scale. I was fascinated. Slowly I tiptoed into the store. I was standing close to the back of the women. I looked up at the scale. Quietly, I moved closer. One woman stepped back on my foot. I screamed from pain and I fled back to the tub. I could hear more laughter. Mom came to finish my bath. The next day, Sunday, the whole neighborhood heard about how George streaked naked in the store. I was five years old. Also, at this time the assembly line bathing routine stopped.

Store Basement

The full basement under the store served for many activities. The huge coal furnace heated the store via floor registers and also heated the living room area. There was a large boarded area where coal was stored. There was a window opening for access to the coal bin.

There was also the toilet in an enclosed area.

One wall had shelves from one end of the basement to the other end. Storage of foodstuffs and packaged goods filled the area.

At one far end there was a huge paper-baling machine. This vise was turned as the paper boxes were smashed down to bundles tied later with wire. Pop sold the bales of paper.

During grape harvest time we had a winery in the far end of the basement. It was fun time for us. Mary, Florence, Mom and I were the official grape stompers. After a bath we each wore short knickers. Entering a large wooden tub with a layer of grapes, we stomped and squeezed the bunches of grapes. As the juice squeezed between out toes, Pop would continue adding plump grapes to the tubs. We ate grapes too. So, purple feet and legs, and purple mouth and chin.

When the tub was filled high with crushed grapes and juice, the tub was carried and emptied into a large vat covered with a colander (sieve) and the juice drained off into the bottom area. The residue of the grapes and stems was squished dry.

The grape liquid had sugar and other ingredients added and was then allowed to ferment. Of course, there were several barrels being allowed to ferment at the same time.

The day arrived when the "cured" liquid became wine. I must have been about ten years old when I helped Pop transfer the wine to larger barrels. Pop stuck a rubber hose into the fermented barrel and sucked the other end of the hose. I was surprised to see the wine come flowing out of the hose. Pop was ready as he now placed the hose into the empty ready barrel, and soon he knew there was enough in the new barrel, so he withdrew the hose. He folded the hose to stop the flow of wine as he moved another empty barrel. He then placed that end of the hose into the new barrel and the flow continued. At times, so as not to lose time, Pop just placed the hose in his mouth, moved a barrel, and then inserted the hose into the new barrel. One day, between moving barrels, Pop handed me the hose to place in my mouth. The wine kept flowing–I kept swallowing. After a few minutes I felt sick. Pop placed the hose into the barrel. I left. I went upstairs and lay down on the family bed. The room was swirling. Pop came up to find me. Why did I stop helping him? He found me. I was sick. I started to retch. Pop laughed. He said I was a drunk. He called Mom from the store. She came with a couple of customers to see what was going on. Mom put her finger into my mouth to my throat and out came the flood of wine into the basin Mom had placed under my chin. My audience laughed and applauded. For weeks after, whenever I visited, the Romanian families offered "the drunk" a drink if I so wanted.

Mom explains all about the early days of the store in her book.

Pop bought a large, round gas stove. A large (brass) kettle, shaped like a half ball with two handles sat in the center opening of the stove. Emma was now the candy maker. She cooked caramel in which she dipped the apples. She placed the dipped apples on a large tray to cool. The aroma filled the entire basement and the aroma floated out the basement windows. The caramel apples sold for ten cents. Of course, all candy bars sold for five cents.

Gas Station

The early 20's brought more cars into Aurora from Chicago and from neighboring cities.

Pigeon Hill needed a gas station, so Pop had a gasoline station pump installed on the High Street curbside of the store. The reservoir gas tank was stored underground. The gas pump had a large round glass container on top of the tall pump. There was this long handle on one side. You actually pumped the handle back and forth to draw the gasoline into the glass container. The container held five gallons of gas. The customer did all the work. He filled his automobile tank; he checked and filled the water radiator, washed his windshield and checked the tires. The early 20's also added new customers because of the gasoline pump. Al Capone and others came from Cicero and Chicago.

Many nights or early mornings Mom or Pop had to arise and wait on someone who needed gas. On several occasions the gangster would fill the tank of his car at 12 cents a gallon, and give Mom a fifty-dollar bill. Off Mom went to our bedroom to the safe. She always had change. I think the gangsters met their match.

We had a couple of known Romanian gangsters. At least that's what people said.

One person was called Crooked Finger Bozga. His left index finger looked as though the middle top section had been cut off. Bozga's left index finger was really crooked. The top half of the finger actually crossed over the middle finger at an angle. It appeared that the middle joint of the index finger had been broken and twisted to the side. The upper joint was also a bit smaller and very tapered toward the fingernail. We all were fascinated. Crooked finger never seemed to mind our curiosity. He never tried to hide that finger. I think we all stared at it. Crooked Finger always dressed up in elegant fashion. He was tall and heavily built. His suits were all tailor-made. His silk ties were pinned with shining jewel stones. The cuffs of his shirts (always sporting jeweled cuff links) hung below the cuff of his jacket sleeve. He always wore gray spats with shining patent shoes.

His father Johan had a farm in the Big Woods area. I wrote a short story about his sad death when we heard about it:

The sow grew meaner and meaner as her time of delivery arrived. Johan went out to the barn for more mash, his movements slow, the same tempo as his thoughts.

"Why hasn't my son come these past weeks? It is difficult for me to feed the pigs. When I was a boy seventy years ago it was fine, but now I'm so tired all the time. I wish my boy were here. Those gangsters are no good for him.

"Why did he have to break his finger as a boy and why didn't the doctor set the finger right? That crooked index finger on his hand was not that bad. And why did everyone call him 'crooked finger?' People are so thoughtless and cruel. I must feed the sow.

"I must tell Crooked Finger Bozga, I mean Liu, that we must sell everything. I will go back to Europe to die."

Absent-mindedly, Johan entered the pigpen. The pigs ran to greet him as he tossed the corn cobs about. He walked toward the sow, trying to step over the slop trough. As he brought his left leg over it, his pant cuff caught on the edge. Headlong he fell screaming in anticipation of the pain that would surely follow.

The sow's reaction was one of fear and survival. She lunged forward toward the prone, still figure. She grunted at the body with her nose, turning the figure over and over. Savagely, she bit at every turn, grunting madly.

When the body did not fight back, the sow angrily ran to the pile of straw. She threw herself down and, with a shriek, gave birth, one after the other, to seven tiny, pink, squirming piglets.

A week later Crooked Finger found what was left of his father. The sow was large and healthy, as were all the little piglets.

Pop had a new gas station with two pumps built in the back lots behind the store. An oil-changing pit was dug just behind the store building. A small office building occupied the edge on the lot. Next to this Pop built a four-car garage. The next lot and the two story, two level house with a large barn on the upper level, completed the property. Pop owned the property from the corner of Pierce Street to the corner of Reising Street.

The gas pumps still had the handle operation for filling the upper gas containers. Customers still pumped and served themselves.

The lower level on Reising Street was rented to a newly arrived Mexican Family. A senor and a senora with their seven-year-old son, Jesus (Isus).

There was no running water yet to the houses on Reising Street. In front of the lower level there was a water pump that pumped up cool, fresh spring water. There was always a drinking ladle there.

On the upper level, just beyond the barn, was the outhouse, a two-seater. In the early 30's the two openings had actual toilet seats there; the kind that are still used on toilets (commodes) today. There are photos of the outhouse, and the two story two level house and the water pump.

The barn became the Barn Theater for all my productions of plays, concerts, and for song and/or dance contests. The Roaring 20's had arrived.

The Barn Theater closed when the upper one bedroom apartment was rented to Mare Gaddis, a retired entertainer from the circus circuit. She was tall and slender, with graceful hands and large black eyes. She was a colored lady. Her dad, Big John, lived with her. I remember the sun tea she always prepared in a large jar. She spooned lots of loose tea, filled the jar with water, placed a cover on the jar, and set the jar out in the sun for the day.

Big John entertained us many an evening in front of the store as the kids sat on the steps. He taught us to tap dance, soft shoe, and shuffling.

Big Theater Barn

A new barn theater was found on Pierce Street in back of a friend's house. It was two stories with the upper level with a full floor. You entered the loft via a hand ladder nailed against the wall. A large size opening led into the theater.

In the 20's there was a live theater at the Fox Theater. There was a troupe of players, the Arthur Gale Players, who presented murder mystery and horror plays. We remember the thunder and lightning, the haunted mansions–windows opening and closing loudly at random, screeching doors opening slowly and screams galore.

I even wrote a play because I was so impressed with the Arthur Gale play, "The Butler Did It." I still have the manuscript–1930?

The jazz age was here. The Fox Theater had Charleston contests. My younger sister and I entered and came in third.

The vaudeville shows were colorful. Dancers, comedians, skits, blackout and fading movie stars in person. Frances X. Bushman appeared as a guest at the Rialto. Our barn theater had more dancers and actors than an audience. Everybody had an act or a talent.

Poor Mom. The new fashions made many of Mom's clothes obsolete. Long ankle length dresses, lace trimming, silk sash belts. Bloomers, corsets, high top lace shoes and buckle shoes. Pumps were in. Short bobbed hair was in. Dresses below the knee, rolled silk stockings. A popular song rang out, "Roll 'em girls, roll 'em girls, roll them down and show your pretty knees." Lucky me! The Barn Theater now had a costume department. We had old lace curtains, which became our stage curtains.

Mom had a large framed photo of her and Pop's wedding. The frame was larger. Behind the frame was a built-in box the full size of the frame. It was about twelve inches deep. Folded carefully in paper was her wedding dress. Her veil was beautifully arranged with the flimsy veil draped around it. In the lower corner were the white wedding shoes. Mom didn't know that this became part of my costume department. This "costume" became a nightmare for me.

Every girl wanted to be a bride. I devised one-act plays. In time every girl was a bride. I didn't worry about size then. Short girls, fat girls, thin and tall–safety pins here, a lifted hem there, tied ribbons everywhere. Sometimes the skirt dragged. Sometimes a wall nail grabbed the gown here and there. The veil suffered more wear and tear.

Mom gingerly climbed the ladder for our big production, "The Bride Goes Wild." The production stopped–Mom saw her wedding gown–the show was over. The theater closed down for a while. I think I got whacked. We loved our theater.

The "B" show had many of the cowboy films. The piano player really made the chase scenes exciting. Admission was 5 cents. A penny bought a piece of candy.

The Strand Theater had the dramas of the day. I still see Lillian Gish in "The White Sister" in the cathedral scene where she walked to the altar. Her hair flowing below the waistline. The servants holding their large oval silver tray. Gently Lillian Gish lays her hair over the tray. Her hair is placed to cover the tray. You see a close-up as these huge scissors cut away long tresses of her hair. Tears flowed as lovely as the tresses.

The serials were very popular. You had to attend the following Saturday. Did the hero/heroine save himself? Did the train wreck? Did she drown? Was she thrown off the cliff? How did they escape? The Strand admission was 10 cents. The movie, a short, a comedy and the news, all for 10 cents.

The Rialto burned down in 1928 while the movie was playing. Roy and I went down into the ruins and he found several rings. His mother came to the store to find out where he got them. I said in the burned out basement. Mom and I, Roy and his mom walked to the downtown police station to return the jewelry. We received a lecture. Later I received a spanking–I was 12 years old.

World War One

The early 20's brought many of the WWI veterans home. The store at Pierce and High corner was a choice location. Across the street, at the northwest corner, there was the streetcar stop going south over the High Street viaduct to downtown Aurora. In cold weather many students and customers waited in our store to wait for the streetcar.

Coming back up High Street the streetcar stopped on the southeast corner. It was at this stop where Mary Ann was hit and dragged by an automobile when she was five years old. We were all coming home from City Park. We all crossed in front of the streetcar. Mary Ann had dashed around the back of the streetcar. Her forehead was hit by the headlight but she had grabbed the top edge of the bumper and she was dragged a short distance. Mom cleaned Mary Ann and Pop drove Mary Ann to St. Charles Hospital. She had a few stitches. A bump on the head had a large bandage. We kids laughed because we thought Mary Ann was wearing a large white hat.

Wintertime was lovely as the guys and gals waited for the streetcar in our store. They all had ice skates strung hanging from their necks. One day, one of the guys said that his friend had placed his tongue to the very cold blade of the skate. The tongue froze to the blade and luckily someone had a thermos of hot coffee. He said that many take a dare and one guy actually ripped his tongue slightly.

Two brothers, both tall and thin, spent many days and hours in the store. They were both shell shocked from WWI. They both smoked. Joe bought a pack of Clown cigarettes, and Jake bought Camels. "They're stronger," he said. They collected cigarette coupons. They traded the coupons for gift items. They gave me some miniature blankets in lovely colors. A series had a state with the state colors printed on each one. Others were designed like American Indian rugs. A few of them are now at the Aurora Historical Museum. Jake said that after the war many American soldiers would use the coupons as money in Europe. Army scrip was being used at that time. Many unsuspecting businesses became victims of this ruse.

Jake told many stories of the war. Everyone learned a few words of French and German. The British English accent that Jake portrayed had us all laughing. We attended many parades downtown on national holidays. We applauded the Civil War veterans as they marched by in their original uniforms. When Jake and Joe marched by with their buddies, we all yelled and applauded harder and more. Decoration Day (now Memorial Day) we all went to the cemetery with flags, large flags, small flags on poles, each with a gold pointed tip. Gravesites of each Civil War and WWI veteran were decorated.

Medicines

There were many folk medicine remedies that were used by the Romanian people. We kids were always being bruised with scraped knees, scraped elbows, and bruised faces. There was a weed called burdock with large leaves. A large leaf was cut to overlay the bruise. The leaf was then soaked wet and rubbed with the homemade soap. This leaf was then applied to the bruised area. On the face gauze was placed over the bruise and taped to hold it. On knees and elbows the leaf was applied and the gauze wrapped around and held with the tape.

My favorite remedy caused me an embarrassment. At the many functions at the Romanian Hall, the mothers always nursed their babies. One method was to chew the soft center of bread. Mixed with the bread were the poppy seeds. Everyone had poppy seeds. When the mixture was well blended the doughy bread was placed in the center of a clean handkerchief. The hanky was then pulled together and twisted to form a small ball at the center. This became the pacifier. This also comforted the teething of the baby. Mom made a poppy seed bread one holiday season. When she became busy in the store, I took some poppy seeds and bread and chewed me a doughy ball. I put it in the center of the hanky. I twisted the hanky. I hid behind the cretonne drapes that hid the sacks of flour on the shelves behind. I sat there and chewed and chewed. My teeth ground holes in the hanky. Mom came to get a sack of flour. She found me with a Romanian pacifier.

I was the star attraction as I sat in a chair, in the middle of the store, chewing on a pacifier. A couple of customers gave me some baby rubber nipples. One gave me a bottle too. The crowning glory was when someone placed a baby bonnet on my head with ribbon ties in pink satin. I think Mom and Pop had a lot more customers that day.

Folk medicine and patent medicine were sold in most grocery and drug stores. Bloodletting was also a therapeutic procedure.

Olar's Romanian Drug Store was on North Root Street next door to the Romanian Hall. On one of the counters there were some large glass jars. Jet-black leaches clung to the sides of the jars. The leaches also known as bloodsuckers would stretch out and up the glass sides. Mr. Olar sold these to customers. He also rented them.

Mom sent me to the drugstore with our own container. I brought six bloodsuckers back home. It was Mom's turn. She put a sweater on backwards so she could have a bare back. My sisters and I watched fascinated. We also peeked while Mom disrobed. As Mom sat on a stool, Pop reached into the container. He pulled out a bloodsucker. He placed it down at the base of Mom's neck. A second bloodsucker went to the lower shoulder, another to the other shoulder, and a fourth one on the middle, lower back. We watched. We giggled. The bloodsuckers were getting fatter and fatter. Soon the leaches had grown long and fat. Pop then pulled very gently but hard to release the bloodsuckers. There were bright red blotches over Mom's back where they had feasted. The remaining two bloodsuckers were placed just beneath the back muscle area below the arms. This "medication" took place twice a year. Did I mention that my pop and my mom are originally from Transylvania in Romania?

Another bloodletting was even more fascinating to watch. Mom's bare back was ready for the other method when bloodsuckers were not available. Small glass cups were prepared for this method. Alcohol was poured and swirled around the inside and then poured out. A match was struck to the inside of the glass cup. A glowing bluish flame engulfed the cup. Immediately the glass cup opening was pressed against Mom's back. Slowly as the flame died, the skin was sucked into the cup. Actually sucked up like a scoop of skin. It looked like half a tennis ball pulled into the cup. The pores now were oozing red blood. As the cup reached near capacity, it was removed carefully.

When we were very young my sisters and I became therapists. We gave therapeutic treatments to Mom and to Pop. Pop would lie on his stomach and I walked up and down his spine. Mom helped me get my balance. I walked slowly putting pressure on my heel, then the ball of my foot as I moved up and then down the spine. When I hit a sore spot, Pop said, "Stop." I stopped, Now, gently push down and up in a bounce! What fun! When I could balance myself, I performed a lot of therapy. The wall helped me when my balance failed me. Mom and Pop enjoyed the "treatments." I had the treatments too, but Pop didn't walk and down my spine. He used the palms of his hand. The treatments on me didn't last long. I was too ticklish!

Mom had stomach surgery. They removed her appendix and a cyst. The cyst was the size of a golf ball. The cyst had the appendix joined to one side. The appendix looked like a chewed piece of gum. Mom brought the cyst/appendix home with her. It was in a beautiful fancy glass container. The cyst was floating in formaldehyde which was a preservative. Emma had her adenoids and her tonsils removed. We all joined in all the ice cream she ate to ease the pain.

I recall in grade school some of us had a vial (small bottle) of mercury. We called it "quick silver." We'd let it drop to splash and separate. It was used in thermometers. The teacher took the mercury away from us. It was too dangerous, she said. She told us that mercury was used in temperature thermometers. We told her that we knew that.

Medicine Shows

Every spring we all enjoyed the Medicine Show. Next door, east of the Indian Creek playground (on Mountain Street) the tent was pitched.

The platform in front of the tent had a large, long table adorned with bottles of elixir and tar with honey liquid. There was a corral next to the stage platform. Enclosed were a pony and a pony cart painted red, white, and blue. There was a pony whip in a leather holder attached to the side of the seat. This was the prize for the child who had entered the contest. But you could only enter if your face had acne. The medication would improve and clear the problem.

The medicine show stayed from one week to two weeks. People came from everywhere. Even from the West Side. The medicine was good for everything; tummy aches, sore throats, colds, dry skin, oily skin, rash, diarrhea and constipation.

My folks sold folk medicine in the store. Their best seller was Tar and Honey cold and sore throat liquid. Lovely bottles. And lovely taste. I loved it. It was 40% alcohol.

The medicine shelves were on the wall at the front display window. All those shelves had glass sliding doors. Pop had a lock put on the folk medicine shelves after I drank almost the whole bottle of that tasty medicine. Now off limits to me.

Well, back to the tent. The barker spieled his speech. The assistants mingled into the crowd with bottles of elixir. They sold dozens of bottles every day. The tent interior had a museum type atmosphere with photos of people's faces, hands, feet, ears and noses. Before and after photos using the medications being sold.

A Romanian boy, Alex, who lived across the street, was the contestant. Roly-poly, a happy soul, he used the medication. The tension built up as a daily announcement kept us all up to date with Alex's progress. The last day everyone was there to see Alex win his prize. He won. The sign did say, "The winner will receive a ride on this beautiful buggy drawn by 'Macaroni the Pony.'" (Pop said that no one ever reads.) Poor Alex. He rode the pony cart all that last day.

Gypsies/Pigeon Hill

The early days following World War I brought the gypsies back to Pigeon Hill. They established their caravans near the hill above Indian Creek, Root Street and Reising Street. They begged and stole their needs.

One day, five of them went to the store. They said the curse would be removed from the store if they were allowed to count all the money in the cash register. Mom screamed "No! No, I'll call the police if you don't leave." But they threatened her all the same. Pop arrived, gave them rations of bacon and potatoes, and asked them to leave. As they left they sang a curse at us. Mom spat back a curse of her own. "Crawl back up your mother's womb." (You will enjoy Mom's version.)

I was very fascinated with the gold button earring the gypsy men wore in the right ear lobe. I visited the beautiful caravan and like the "Beware the proverbial gypsy who carried gifts," I brought some items from "my" grocery store. I was told by the gypsy men that the gold button was worn because the gold was good for the eyes. The eyes would always be strong. My folks would not allow me to have my ear pierced. But Mom gave me a ten dollar gold piece, which she said was just as good. Just rub the coin every day. "But where?" I asked. "On my ears?" Mom never answered me.

The gypsies suddenly were no more. They disappeared shortly after Marika's mother wandered wildly up Pierce Street screaming "Where's my daughter, where's Marika?" She was tearing at her hair and her tears stained her face.

They found Marika at the Indian Creek Playground. Marika was seven years old.

Also at this time, my sister Mary Ann suddenly had her appendix operation at St. Charles Hospital. Mary Ann, as you know, had been a breech baby. She was retarded. With all the whispering I heard what really happened. Mary Ann was "fixed" not to have a baby. I asked Mom. She said that with the Lindberg kidnapping and bad people around, it was the best thing to do for Mary.

Superstitions-Mail Orders

Emma came home from church one Sunday very upset. She was now a teenager. Emma felt another young girl staring at her. Emma looked at the girl who did not move but kept staring. Emma felt the hair rise on her neck as a cold shiver rushed through her. She had been bewitched with an "evil eye." Mom tried to pacify her feelings. Emma always felt she was bewitched.

Mom always said that it is worse to be hit by mouth than to be hit by hand. Well, to be hit by a broom is the worst. If a young man is hit by a broom intentionally, it is believed that his wife will go insane on their wedding day.

Speaking of brooms. On special Sundays, Mom and Pop both went to High Mass at 10 a.m. Mary, Emma, and Florence also attended. I was 12 years old, so I was left to tend the store. There were really only one or two customers, as everyone was in church. I had attended early Mass, which I preferred. It only lasted an hour. I was sitting behind the cigar counter at the front window, daydreaming.

Suddenly I heard this screaming and yelling coming from across the street. I went to the front door, opened the screen door and stepped out to have a look. There, across the street, "Katy corner" was Mrs. Bodescue beating Mr. Bodescue on his head and shoulders and back with a broom. She kept beating and beating as he ran back and forth down the front yard and back up the porch and down again. The Romanian swear words are really beautiful. Mingled with the cuss words are spoken thoughts of every wrong ever done and said. Mr. Bodescue finally went into the house. Quiet and peace returned. Mr. Bodescue never drank again. He never slapped Mrs. Bodescue again. Mrs. Bodescue even dressed up that Sunday and walked the two blocks to church. She was late of course. I'm sure she was in time for confession and communion.

Poor Litra, their teenage daughter. She had a hooknose and her lower jaw was protruded. Her lower teeth extended just beyond the upper teeth. Beautiful blond hair now cut in the new flapper look helped set off her bright green cat eyes. She and I were magazine addicts. Movie magazines, Billboard Magazine, Liberty, Health and Fitness books, Benard McFaden, Atlas. We sent away for everything. Charles Atlas taught me to flex my muscles. Benard McFaden taught me to brush my tongue too, when I brushed my teeth.

I misread and misinterpreted the article about eyes. I thought if you ate carrots your eyes would become blue in color. I had dark brown eyes. I loved blue eyes. Poor Mom—I pulled fresh carrots from our garden, rubbed the dirt off on my pants, and ate raw carrots. I ate carrot slaw, made carrot juice. My eyes are still brown.

We sent away for a "nose straightener." A metal beautiful Roman shaped nosepiece. The piece had a flat hole at the top and three slits on each side of the length of the nose. Beaded through each slit was the tape string hanging out to a half dollar size double ring attachment. The tapes all were pushed through the ring ready to be adjusted. You placed the nosepiece over your nose. The top tape went over your head to the large double slotted ring, which would rest in the center at the back of the head. The other tapes, three on each side of the nosepiece, would stretch under the top of the ear, two under the ear, and three at an angle across the jaw. When all is in place, you pull each tape until it is snug. You then pull as tightly as you can. You wear this overnight while you sleep. After a few nights, a newly shaped nose.

I helped Litra one Friday night. She sneaked home. We waited for Saturday. Eek! Saturday morning we removed the nosepiece. Litra's nose was black and blue. Her cheeks and upper lip were black and blue. Her eyes were black and blue. Her mother asked, "Who did this?" Litra said, "George bought it." My pop asked me "Where'd you get the money?" I said the cash register. I remember going to the basement. I remember that razor strap. I remember my black and blue ass. I didn't know that the cash register had a lock, because after this I could not open the register.

Meanwhile, one more superstition. When Pop had the new electric walk-in refrigerator placed in the corner of the store, there was room for storage above the icebox. The new refrigerator reached about three feet below the ceiling. So there was all that room for boxes and baskets.

One day Emma started to scream. We all happened to be at home/store. She scared the hell out of us. "What is it? What happened?" There sitting on the top corner of the new fridge was a large black bird with shiny white eyes flashing. Emma crossed herself, Mom crossed herself, and I asked "What?" "If a bird flies in your home that means that someone will die." When you see a bird in the house you cross yourself and you utter a prayer. We all crossed ourselves. We waited. Days went by. Weeks went by. Oh, we chased the bird out of the store with a broom. We literally scared the shit out of that poor bird. Yes, we actually did. No one died.

Florence also worked in the store as a child. One day she waited on a man at the cigar counter. He took out his coin purse, opened it, and as Florence watched the man's face, his one eye looked at the purse and the other eye stared at Florence. She said nothing but she was frightened. We learned that the man had a glass eye. A WWI injury.

Poor Mary Ann had a bedwetting problem and a seepage problem in her black bloomers. I recall another incident one early evening. Poor Mary! Poor us! We were seated around the radio when Mary went to the basement to the toilet. When she came back Mom checked and found damp bloomers. Mom went to the top landing to the cellar. She returned with an old broom. She put a few drops of kerosene on the broom and put a match to it. The flames spread swiftly. Mom shook the broom toward Mary who ran around the table as Mom chased her with the burning broom. This was believed to frighten a person to not pee in their pants. Florence and I watched wide-eyed. We all peed in our pants. Mom never burned the broom again.

Thunder and lightning storms always frightened us. Sometimes during a storm, the sun would suddenly shine through a cloud. It was said that when the sun shines during a storm, the Devil is beating his wife.

The bad hour. It was said that you should never wish another person ill wishes or make a bad remark. We have "one bad hour" during each day. This bad hour reverses any bad wish made about another person. And the bad wish falls on you.

When the Gypsies were in our store, they brought out an egg. They wanted Pop to put up five dollars to check his good luck. Pop said "no." The Gypsies finally said one dollar. "Okay," Pop said. They had a tin cup and they broke the egg into it. "Ohh," they moaned. "The egg has blood in it. That's bad luck. For five dollars we can cast a spell over it. You will then always have 'good luck.'" Mom arrived. The Gypsies fled. Pop got drunk.

The Hobo Jungle

Walking down Pierce Street you cross Broadway and continue down a dirt roadway to the Fox River. There are many trees and high shrubs as you enter a pathway. This pathway leads into a larger clear area with makeshift tents of corrugated tin and packing cardboard boxes. Around the semi-circular area are circles of stones and rocks for the half-dozen or more campfire sites. This is the Hobo Jungle. You can always smell brewing coffee in old coffee cans. Fish fries make your stomach growl. Fresh dug Indian potatoes are cooking under the embers of the glowing small logs and branches. There's even the glow of coals.

Here you'll see and meet our own Romanian Hobo–"Pork Chops." Short and stocky with a round cherubic face, flashing black eyes shaded with thick black brows and a full thick mouth. The outer edges of the lips always seem to be turned up to pose an amused smile. Black hair, full and curly. Pork Chops was always immaculately dressed. Shiny threadbare pants. Clean gray stained shirts, always a tie. Sometimes a vest. Ankle high laced black shoes. Never without a hat. On Sundays or special days Pork Chops wore a black derby. His felt hats were black, brown or gray.

We often wondered where he kept all these hats. We never found out. I think in the cold months Pork Chops went south with the birds. We saw him only in spring and in the summer. He was a frequent "customer" at our store.

Always on his grocery list was the small tin of "canned heat" (Sterno), which was a luxury at 10 cents a can. The hobos would melt the contents of the "canned heat" to a clear pink liquid. They placed and boiled the potatoes in the mixture. The potatoes were said to draw out the poisons of the mixture. The remaining liquid was now 100% alcohol. The hobos drank this alcohol. Sadly, some became very ill. One incident killed a hobo. The potatoes used in the mixture were always smashed and buried far away from the Hobo Camp. I remember once I told my pop that I tasted the "canned heat." He refused to sell any more to the hobos. I was 9 years old.

    Pork Chops lived in the Hobo Jungle for many years. He died in the early '30's. The Romanian community gave him a beautiful funeral. I cried. I loved Pork Chop. He told us wonderful stories. His youth, his marriage, his two children, his work, and the tragic deaths of his entire family. The hobos made a lovely memorial cross which was placed on the banks of the Fox River, next to the Hobo Jungle.

Election Day and the Grocery Store

The voting polls on Pigeon Hill were at our store. The four voting booths were always placed in front of the dry goods counter. The candidates in the election and their committees milled around outside on the sidewalks. They handed out business size cards that contained their photo and the printed message of the office for which they were running. They were very friendly and spoke to all the voters. The candidates went from one polling place to another all day long. Pigeon Hill had a lot of voters and a large German population. Occasionally the Pigeon Hill area produced a candidate for office. This really created excitement.

Our store was a busy place. Our customers included many of the residents of Pigeon Hill. The Romanians, Hungarians and Germans who traded at our store also had charge accounts.

The German grocery store, Brown's, was across the street. East of us, a half block away, was Fiji Hungarian Store. A block south of Pierce Street and a block north next to the Romanian Hall was Frunzar's Romanian/Hungarian Grocery Store. Next door across the alley from the Romanian Hall was Olar's Romanian Drug Store.

As a child I was always surprised to see the owners of these stores coming in to vote at our store. We saw everyone from the hill. Of course, all our customers did their shopping too.

Up from Pierce Street on Lincoln Avenue was the Szilagyi grocery store. It was located across the alley from the Romanian Church.

Bootlegging and Whiskey

The raid took place at night in northeast Aurora on Pigeon Hill. The deputy sheriffs raided the home of Joe DeKing after they were driven away earlier. The raiding party entered the house with a warrant. Mr. DeKing was in bed. His wife Lillian was asked if they had liquor. She said yes and walked the Sheriff and party to the kitchen. There was a half-pint of whiskey. Joe DeKing arrived. He had a gun. The other raiders came up from the basement carrying wine bottles. An argument ensued.

The Sheriff clubbed Joe DeKing with a shotgun. Mr. DeKing dropped his gun. Mrs. DeKing picked up the gun. The Sheriff's shotgun went off. A round from the shotgun killed Mrs. DeKing. The son, Gerald, picked up the gun from his mother's side. He fired. He shot one of the Sheriffs who was hospitalized. He recovered. The jury did not indict Joe DeKing. President Hoover said it was not a federal thing, but a local thing.

The late 20's brought out many raiding parties of deputy Sheriffs. Most grocery stores and business people who had bars, pool halls, and card playing parlors were targeted. I believe that people were allowed a pint of whisky for medicinal needs with a prescription by a doctor. There were only certain legalized places to fill this prescription. But there were bootleggers everywhere.

I remember a tug-of-war and words when I was about seven years old. Mom was at the store. She was talking to some strange man. Mom was holding a half-empty whisky bottle. The man was trying to take it away from Mom. She refused to let go. She explained and told him to call the doctor. He finally left without the bottle. Everyone learned to never give up that bottle. For medicinal purposes. Yes! I remember wintertime. After our baths, we were rubbed with hot goose fat, melted and blended with eucalyptus oil, alcohol and other smelly ingredients. Our chests were wrapped with flannel. Then that wonderful "medication." We were served a steaming hot cup of Mom's hot toddy. Mmmmm! Melted goose fat, ½ shot of whiskey, some honey or sugar and hot water. Off to bed we drifted, glowing inside and out.

Murder

Mom and Pop married on September 22, 1911. That following week they rented a boarding house. Boarders were plenty. Mom started her work two days after the wedding. There were several boarding houses on Broadway. They were all located across the street from the Roundhouse, and north to and beyond Pierce Street. A Romanian family had a grocery store there too.

A few months before Mom and Pop rented the boarding house a murder took place near these boarding houses. The girl named Flora S. had met George K. at one of these houses where they were boarders. He was 19, she was 16. They fell in love. They planned to elope to Geneva or some other close town. They both worked at the Aurora Cotton Mills.

On September 7th a foot of snow covered the City of Aurora.

George and Flora planned to meet September 8th after work, about 6 p.m. They met on the New York Street Bridge. When they met, he asked her for five dollars so he could retrieve a watch from the repair shop. Flora had withdrawn over one hundred dollars from the bank. George went to a hardware store and bought a gun.

They walked to the depot. George said he hadn't checked the train schedule and maybe there were no more trains coming. He suggested that they walk the six miles. They walked along the tracks, plowing through two feet of snow. They walked to the North Aurora area when he asked Flora to walk ahead of him. After she went several feet, George started shooting. Three bullets struck her, one in her neck and the others in her body. He took her money as she lay there in the snow. He threw away the gun. He ran back to his mother's home.

Flora crawled for over a mile through the snowdrifts. A watchman found her near the Chemical Works. Flora was taken to St. Charles Hospital. The police were called. George was in bed at home. George was arrested. He claimed that he and Flora had decided to fulfill a suicide pact. At the hospital George was allowed to visit with Flora. In one corner behind the curtained area, there were two Romanian interpreters. George begged forgiveness from Flora. Flora died four days later. George was sent to Joliet Prison. He was paroled in 1926. George married a lady friend and they made their home in Joliet.

In 1930, George, his wife and their one year old daughter were enroute home. They had been to a church bazaar in Aurora. Just southwest of Joliet they were approaching the Chicago and Northwestern rail crossing. The police thought that perhaps he hadn't heard the whistle. All three were killed at the crossing.

Leg Accident

I didn't see the car turn the corner as I ran across High Street. As I reached the curb my right foot slammed into the wire spokes of the rear wheel. My body twisted as the wheel carried me around and flipped me loose into the air. My body hurled into the wires above, dangled for a moment, and then fell down to the curb. A neighbor carried me into the store. My long black stocking on my right leg was starting to balloon around the ankle area. I reached to feel it and the blood started to ooze. I cried as my mother held me. She said the doctor was on his way. If I stopped crying, she said she'd give me an Eskimo Pie. She brought me a silver foiled ice cream bar. "What's that?" I asked. "I want a pie," I cried. The doctor arrived.

I loved the St. Charles Hospital. Everyone brought baskets of fruit and candy. "For display only," the nurse said. One evening I sneaked a Tango chocolate bar. The nurse caught me. She said I was bad. I felt sick, and threw up on the nurse. I was happy. I was nine years old.

For two days my leg was wrapped in ice. The doctor said a new method of repair to the compound fracture would be tried. This would prevent the leg from amputation. My mom and pop agreed. Everyone wrote on the plaster cast. I loved the hospital. There was a large, half circle cradle over my leg. Two weeks later they sent me home. I spent my time in the yard next to the store. The customers from the store stopped to visit and to bring toys and goodies. I loved the yard. I also had a long leather change purse. It filled quickly with coins and paper bills. My money disappeared one day. Shortly after this, in 1926, my mom went to visit Romania. I still had my empty purse.

Exercise, the doctor told my mom. So I became a member of the YMCA. A huge swimming pool and gymnasium gave me all the exercise to strengthen my leg, now an inch longer than my left leg.

The YMCA was for boys and for men. All swimming was in the nude. We learned backhand, to swim on our backs, to float, to dive. When classes were over we played games. One game was sinking our bodies under the water on our backsides, then suddenly thrust our midsection up and yell "WEENIE ON THE TABLE."

I was also enrolled in a dancing school. I was the only boy. I was a tall boy. The teacher paired me with a short girl. I plied, I jumped, I skipped, and I did an entrechat. My arms were up, my arms were down, my hands were bent, and my hands were straight. So this was ballet. My new clog shoes danced the time step, the double time, and on sand. My four-year-old sister, Florence, started classes. I had a partner. She was tall.

Boy Scouts

Boy Scout Troop #19 held meetings in Indian Creek School, at High Street and Mountain Street. The Indian Creek Library was also located there. The troop had scouts from all the families of Pigeon Hill. We were a mixture of Romanians, Luxemburgers, Germans, and Hungarians.

Specks was our scoutmaster. Our uniforms included the brown, olive colored wraparound leggings. We camped out. We learned all the things Boy Scouts learn. We worked for the many awards. We had fun. We loved the camp in the Michigan sand dunes. We had the best areas all around Aurora, The Fox River. The Indian trips to Starved Rock. The trip to learn sailing when we became Sea Scouts at Lake Michigan. We actually met an Indian Chief. He taught us Indian culture. He showed me a ceremonial Indian dance. He honored me when he loaned me an Indian costume and a Chief's feathered headdress. The feathers cascaded down my back almost to the floor.

The great moment in scouting was the huge International Scout Jamboree held in Windsor, Canada. We bussed to Detroit. Ah–those barrels of Vernor's Root Beer at the waterfront. The world's best. The marching parades. The scout uniforms and hats of other countries. The friendships.

While we took a ferry back to Detroit from Windsor I had an ink sketch drawn by the young artist. He charged 25 cents for a profile sketch. I didn't like my profile. So for 50 cents he would do a full-face sketch. In 1930, 50 cents was a lot of money. But my dad had a cash register. And I had 50 cents.

Before we landed in Detroit the artist sought me out. He had a young couple with him. In his hand he had a sketch pad. The sketch was a full-face of the young lady. The artist asked me to tell the young couple how much I had paid for the full-face sketch. I said 50 cents. They all left me to myself. I was learning life everywhere. The sketch is here. I'll call it "My 50 cents sketch."

My 50 cent charcoal sketch
Boy Scout Jamboree
Lake Michigan
1931

Sport Times and Sad Times

1924 Red Grange, "The Galloping Ghost" excited us all with his football feats.

1925 Floyd Collins died in a cave as passage is obstructed. Our family visited Uncle George in Chicago. We kids played and pumped the player piano on and on. One of our favorite piano music rolls was titled "The Death of Floyd Collins."

1926 Valentino died on August 23rd. The headlines ran for days in all the newspapers. In the 30's, when the family moved to Los Angeles, we visited the Hollywood Cemetery. We met the caretaker, and he gave us a tour of the entire cemetery. He then brought out a very tattered huge wreath, designed entirely of beautiful small multi-colored beads. He gave each of us, Mom and Pop, Mary, Florence and me a few beads from the wreath. The wreath of beaded flowers came from Mussolini.

1927 All the boys got a "Gene Tunney" haircut. Gene Tunney knocked out Jack Dempsey. People were upset because of "the long count."

1928 Richard E. Byrd planted our U.S. flag on the South Pole.

1929 Stock market crash.

1930 Center School- "Junior High"

1930 Airplane ride. Mom and I took our first airplane ride at North Aurora Airport on June 1st.

1931 East High.

1923 to Calvin Coolidge died January 5, 1933. His widow wore white at 1929 the funeral. Everyone talked about it.

The 20's were very exciting. Lindberg's plane flew over Aurora. The Graf Zeppelin flew over Aurora. The stock market crashed. I remember Mom's often used remark, "The pillow's been snatched from under the Gypsy's ass." The gangster era exploded with the Saint Valentine's Massacre. The 30's arrived with the depression.

Walkathons played in many cities. Our North Aurora Fairgrounds Walkathon was attended by everyone. Certain couples became favorites. People were giving

parachute shows. Anyone could jump and you were paid $20.00. In 1932, a young girl, Ruth York, jumped to her death, the chute did not open.

There was a shooting at Saint Michael's Hall on Rural Street. The bar and two alley bowling was crowded this weekend. One injured. Two or three people were killed by the train under the High Street Bridge. Gruesome sight to school kids enroute to classes.

The night before Mom went to Europe (1927) a car speeding over the High Street Bridge suddenly flipped end over end. It landed upside down near the gas station. The two occupants were taken to St. Charles Hospital. They were gone.

Typical funeral at St. Michael's Church
1925
Mrs. Alex (Marika) Trippon, deceased

Romanian funeral in the 1920's
Reverend Vuc officiating

First St. Michael's Church
1916 funeral of soldier cousin
On left: Mom with hat holding George, Pop holding Mary Ann
and Emma standing next to Mom (note Emma's hat).

Funeral, circa 1920, St. Michael's Church
Reverend Mann officiating

Romanian Christmas and the Vitfliam with church elders (circa 1918)
Pop Trippon is to right of Moshua with large moustache.
To Pop's right is Mr. F. Trense.

George W. Trippon and Mary Trippon 59

1936 funeral at home of deceased.
Emma and the Trense Family behind the coffin.

The Casa Romana was the social center for the Romanian Colony. The upper floor had a full ballroom. At the far end there was a stage with dressing room. The basement had a long full bar on one side. There was a two-lane bowling alley on the opposite wall. Most weddings, receptions and dancing parties were enjoyed here. Special plays and events were also produced here. To the south of the Casa Romana was an alley. At the other end of the alley was the church school property and the church.

Mom—18 years old
Cleveland, Ohio
1910

George W. Trippon and Mary Trippon

Mary Szilagyi & George Trippon
Wedding Day
September 22, 1911

Mom and Pop's Wedding Party
September 22, 1911

Note the arrangement of the wedding veil in the fashion of Romanian brides.

For a boutonniere the groom wears a sprig of rosemary, an aromatic herb which a Romanian girl combines with an artificial flower and gives to the man of her choice to wear to Saturday night mass. He places it in his hat band and proudly holds his hat so that all may see as he precedes the girl down the aisle of the church. In this way, they announce their preference for each other, and a wedding soon follows. Note the rosettes with long streamers which the ushers wear. The men also wear rosettes and streamers on their hats. As friends and relatives assemble at the church for the wedding, the ushers often dance and sing before they seat the people who are arriving. It is an old Romanian custom.

Mom and Pop as Best Man and Maid of Honor
(Mom holding Emma) at
cousin John Silagyi's wedding.
Circa 1912

Mom on extreme left at George Pop's wedding.
Pop at right with Emma sitting in front of him.
Girl in plaid is Mary Burson.
Circa 1914

Emma TrIppon and Victor Trense Wedding, 1931
Fifteen Bridesmaids

At left Mr. & Mrs. George Moldovon (Mary Burson Maldovon can be seen in photo of George Pop's wedding, Circa 1914

Emma and Vic's wedding party
of friends and relatives

The Trippon Grocery Store at
corner of Pierce and High Streets.
Note the cement steps. There was a side
entrance to the store and a large window.

Note: became a member of Royal Blue Store to compete with
newly opened chain grocery store "Consumer" on Pigeon Hill, in
the early '30's. Note basement windows: 1st window–wine cellar;
2nd window–coal bin; 3rd window–work area and toilet.

Pop's Grocery Store, Aurora, Illinois–1922

Grocery Store, Aurora, Illinois–late 1920's
Mom and Florence at right

Mary, Mom, Mr. Frisch, Florence, Ann, George, Laura, Fagie
Pop's Grocery Store, Aurora, Illinois–1935

Front   Reverse
Billing books for credit sales menu–1920's

The Trippon Grocery Store, circa 1930,
first gas station on Pigeon Hill.
The new pump gas station on High Street at back of grocery store. Three-car garage and office building. Annie Kuk, Florence Trippon, George Trippon and Morton Hollis, mechanic and attendant of pumps. Note the oil change pit to the right. The delivery truck and the old Dodge with Pop sitting in the front seat. Chimney in background (above truck) is the Reising Street house.

George W. Trippon and Mary Trippon 71

The garage and gas station on Pigeon Hill–High Street and Pierce Street.
Note: gas pumps were removed; now repair shop.
Circa 1933
Note St. Michael's Church steeple in background.

The Reising Street two story house. Top floor: two bedrooms. Lower floor: one bedroom.
Fireplace, no running water (note lady pumping water from well). No toilet (see below). Notice
St. Michael's Church Steeple.

Circa 1933

The last outhouse on Pigeon Hill
on High Street above Reising Street

Pop at extreme left on 2nd row in front of large lamp.
To right of #644 is George Pop sitting down.
CB&Q Railroad–Aurora, Illinois
Circa 1916/1917

The Roundhouse, south of Pierce Street on Broadway.
Pop worked in the railroad yards east of the Roundhouse.
(later photo)

Pop (George Trippon) & younger brother
Circa 1910

George W. Trippon and Mary Trippon

Brother Ambrose Trippon,
younger brother & Pop (George Trippon)
Circa 1910

Pop (George Trippon)
Uncle Ambrose & Uncle Mihai Trippon
Circa 1913

Uncle Ambrose and Pop
(George Trippon)
Circa 1910

Baby Marika
1914
Aurora, Illinois

 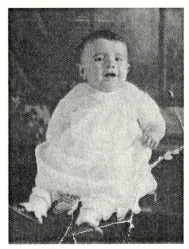

George W. Trippon
1916
Aurora, Illinois

Mary, George, Emma Trippon
Aurora, Illinois
1916

George and Cousin Bill Szilagyi
Aurora, Illinois
1916

George and Mary Trippon
with Emma and Baby Mary
Aurora, Illinois
1914

Mary and George Trippon and
their three older children
Emma, Mary and George
Aurora, Illinois
1917

Circa 1924
Born
Emma 1912
Mary 1914
George 1916
Florence 1918
Aurora, Illinois

Notice Emma's new "bobbed hair do" and flapper dress! Note Florence's stockings with frilly bands.

Emma, George, Mary, Florence
1924
Aurora, Illinois

Mary Trippon & her four children
1920
Mary, Emma, Mom, Florence, George
(Note embroidered blouses)

Brady School
1927
My new cap.

Mary Ann
St. Michael's School
1926

My trombone –1927
Note the laced shoes and the
Rose pinned to my red tie!

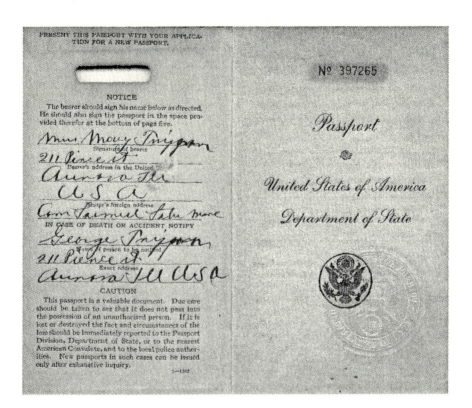

Mom's 1927 Passport
Note old address number *211* Pierce
changed to *425*

Mom's 1927 Passport

Mom with new
Bobbed hair and shorter dress
1926

Circa 1928-1929 (Aurora, Illinois)

Maria on left. Rosie on right. Married to Manual Lopez. Lived on North Broadway, about four blocks toward town from Pierce Street. In the late '20's, this area became inhabited by the new Mexican labor at CB&Q. The area also had a few whorehouses.

Originally, in the early '20's, most of the residents were Romanian. Mom and Pop had their boarding house on Broadway, too. The original Pink's Grocery Store was in that area also.

Perhaps you can recall Emma telling of her frightful experience one day with Rosie? She drove Rosie, with her groceries, to her home on Broadway.

When Emma stopped in front of Rosie's house, there was Maria on the porch embracing Manual. Rosie pulled out a gun, got out of the car, screaming "Bitch!" etc., firing the gun several times. Scared the Hell out of Emma. She sped off like mad. Pop and Mom had quite a time consoling the hysterical Emma.

Emma refused to deliver any more orders. I was about 13 or 14 years old at the time. Pop taught me to drive and I became the Delivery Person.

Rosie did shoot Manual. He recovered. Maria was deported. Rosie went to prison. They still owe for the groceries.

......this is Mom's story

Mom's 95th Birthday
Hollywood, California
1987

Mom's Story

Coming to America

After my grandfathers died, we had a difficult time. Taxes grew higher and work was hard to get. Money and food were scarce. At that time, the United States of America had lax immigration laws and no "quotas." Almost everyone who could pay for a ticket could secure a passport to America and our Romanian men went in droves, sending for them later or else of returning to Romania to buy more land, thus attaining more prestige and influence in the community.

For a long while, my father talked about going to the United States. His dream was to work and save money, return and pay all our debts, and buy more land. Mother, who was passionately attached to Romanian soil, shares this dream and was willing for Father to go. They sold their livestock and scrimped and saved to get money for his ticket. Finally, he had enough money for the journey. The year was 1905.

One morning, in late summer, with his precious passport and ticket safely in his pocket, he left with twelve or fifteen of his countrymen for America, the land of which he had dreamed of so long.

Mother explained that we couldn't all go to Satu Mare to see Father off on the train. Someone would have to stay and look after the place. So we kissed Father goodbye at him and watched him drive away with Mother in the wagon. He had his bundle of clothes and a large linen bag filled with enough food to last him until he reached America.

When Mother returned, she was very quiet and I could see that she had been crying. But there were no tears when she called her children to her. She said that we must work hard so that things would go well while Father was away, and that we must pray every day that he would be cared for and protected wherever he might be and that, some day, he would come safely back to us. We prayed with intensity and fervor.

Each Tuesday for nine weeks straight, Mother sent us to the attic without breakfast to pray the whole Rosary. We would almost cry with hunger. At twelve o'clock, we would have a slice of bread and a small bowl of soup and go again to the attic to pray. After the sun went down and the stars came out, Mother would give us supper. For us, it was something like a novena, but Mother herself continued to fast and pray almost every Tuesday.

Mother also decided to go to Bigsod to the annual prayer meeting and left George, Julia and me at home to look after things. We were not really alone because Aunt Traiji (Romanian for Theresa), Mother's sister, and her family lived in the back room.

Mother gave us many instructions before she left, especially about our religious duties. We must not eat bacon or mild or eggs before St. Mary's day, but instead, I must cook beans, potatoes, mushrooms, and sauerkraut. On Holy Day we must not eat breakfast, but must fast until after the church services.

We carried out Mother's instructions to the letter and, when we got home from church, we were very hungry. We were going to have bacon. I was slicing the bacon, but George didn't think I was working fast enough. He was hungry.

He grabbed a knife from my hand and I received a cut between my thumb and forefinger that was almost to the bone. The blood began to spurt and I began to scream and cry. Uncle John heard and came running in. When he saw what had happened he grabbed a handful of salt and held it over the wound. The blood stopped spurting and, in about five minutes, the bleeding stopped. We still use salt in our household to stop the flow of blood from a cut, but we never use spider webs for that purpose as the neighbor did when I cut my foot on the glass bottle.

When Father reached America, he went first to Pennsylvania with some of his countrymen and worked in a coal mine. Since he could neither read nor write, he had to get others to write letters for him. He sent us money several times and then he had someone write us that he was going to Wyoming to herd sheep. For several years after, we heard nothing from him. We didn't know whether he was alive or dead.

In the meantime, my older brother, Dan, had also gone to America and found work in a steel mill in East Chicago, Indiana. We heard from Dan, but he had not heard anything from Father.

Mother, George, Julia and I got along as best we could. At first, I stayed at home with George and Julia while Mother went out to work, too. I hoed corn, sunflowers, and potatoes with a large, heavy hoe. The hoeing season lasted from twenty to twenty-five days.

We took our lunch with us. We were paid from ten to fifteen cents a day, but even this was a great help to the family. If two or three children were working, their combined earnings would total between two and three dollars by the end of the week. That was a lot of money and it was used to buy necessities like salt, vinegar and kerosene for the lamp. These things we would not otherwise have had.

Another fall job for which we received small but needed pay was picking oak leaves in the woods to feed the sheep.

In a village where the houses have roofs of straw and where there are great stacks of hay about the premises, fire is naturally a great hazard. One of the main duties of our village night watchman was to look out for fires. It was a catastrophe for a fire to get started, because there were such poor facilities for fire fighting. But a fire did get started and wrought havoc in our village.

We children were in the woods picking oak leaves for the sheep when we saw a big column of smoke rising from the direction of our village. We were quite a distance away, but we dropped everything and ran home as fast as we could.

When we reached tee village, we found that our own home had burned and only the adobe walls were standing. I ran through the yard where the hot ashes from the wheat stack burned my feet. At first, I couldn't see Mother and ran wildly about looking for her. I found her crying out in the back acreage.

We were almost overwhelmed by the calamity that had befallen us and our friends and neighbors. The fire department had come from Satu Mare, but the fire had spread from straw roof to haystack. It burned for three days before it finally burned itself out. When the smoke died down, more than half of the village was gone.

We later learned that two young brothers, who had been left at home while the older people in the family were at work in the harvest, had been playing with matches and got the fire started.

We faced a double calamity: our homes were lost and most of the peasants lost their year's crop. We were among the number. We had just finished threshing our wheat and piled in our house were fifteen or twenty homespun sacks filled with wheat waiting to be sold to pay our taxes and to be ground for our year's supply of bread. Each sack held four bushels of wheat. When Mother saw the fire and realized our home was in its path, she tried to move the sacks of wheat to safety. But they were tied with rope at the tip and were too heavy for her to lift. She managed to open four of the sacks and to empty out enough wheat to be able to drag the sacks out into the acreage at the back of the house. These four part-sacks were all the wheat that was saved from the fire. Mother also saved a few of our clothes, but none of the furniture. We didn't even have a spoon or a fork with which to eat.

For three nights, we slept out in the acreage, hardly knowing what to do or where to turn. The smoke hung over the village like a pall; so dense it almost smothered us.

When the fire caught, Mother had untied the calf at the barn and had turned it loose. After the smoke began to clear, she told us to look around to see if we could find the calf. I finally located it tied to a lady's back fence.

When I asked her about the calf, she said she had found it wandering about and, not knowing to whom it belonged, had tied it up and looked after it. She asked if we had a place to move. I told her we had none and that we had been sleeping out in the field for the last three nights.

She said, "Go back and talk to your mother. She can move over here and live in my back room. I'll charge her ten dollars a year rent."

My mother went to see this lady and we arranged to move in with her.

Already, however, my mother was thinking and planning how she could build another house. She had started to look around for the necessary lumber. The adobe walls of or house were still standing, but they had been so weakened that they had to be rebuilt.

Aunt Traiji and her family had shared the house that had burned, but there had been some friction between the two families. When different friends heard that Mother was planning another house, they urged her to build for her own family and not plan a house that would again have to be shared.

My mother was a woman of decision. She felt that the advice to build a separate house was sound and laid her plans accordingly. She planned a kitchen with a living room on either side, a storage room and barn, and a nice pig house at the back with stairs leading into the attic for the chickens to stay in winter.

About this time, the "yager" in charge of the woods came to see my mother. A yager's duties were something like those of a forest ranger and, each year, the people of the village were entitled to a certain amount of wood. The yager had been a good friend of my grandfather and now he told Mother, "Annie, if you want to build a house, I will let you have the wood that you need."

So we procured the timbers we needed and Mother, George and I started to build the house. Julia, our baby sister, was too small to help. It was then that "bread" Grandfather Szilagyi "had cast upon the waters" was returned to us.

Some Hungarians who lived in a distant village heard of our misfortune. They remembered how Grandfather had always opened his place to them when they carried their produce to market and how he never failed to have a friendly greeting for them. They came and donated work with their horses in mixing part of the adobe.

The Hungarians have wonderful help, but much of the adobe we made ourselves, and used our feet to mix it. I shall never forget how hard we worked, my mother, George and I. It took us about a year to build our new home. We began it during Lent when we were on a starvation diet of dry bread and salted herring.

Mother had borrowed a few bushels of wheat so we could exist until the next crop was harvested and she had had to borrow money to pay taxes. We worked so hard and ate so little, that it affected our vision. By the time Easter came, we were so blind we couldn't find our way at night. Our vision came back after we recuperated from our starvation diet and our hard work.

It was while we were living with the lady who found the calf, that I added to the complications by getting an infection in my leg that settled in my heel. For a long time, I couldn't walk. During the day, Mother would take me out to lie on the porch.

One day, she had about six ladies helping her beat rye straw for the roof of our new house when a thunderstorm came up. They were trying to gather up the rye grains from the hard ground before the rain came and were working so hard that they didn't have time to put me back in the house.

The rain began pelting down and suddenly lightening struck a tree right next door. I was so frightened I forgot all about my sore leg and heel and started to run. Mother caught me and brought me back to bed.

Finally, I recovered from the infection and was able to carry my share of work and responsibility. By the time I was fifteen years old, in 1915, I was able to pick up wheat and tie it in bundles as fast as a man could cut it, no matter how hard he worked. Also, I was strong enough to lift a three-bushel bag of wheat to my shoulder and put it in the wagon.

Yanco Stirs the Fire

According to Romanian standards, I was getting old enough to marry. I was fifteen and most Romanian girls marry between that age and twenty. Since I had learned to spin and weave and carry on the work of the household, I was considered ready to preside over a home of my own. I was, therefore, permitted to attend the dances, a sign that I was of marriageable age.

My dowry chest was properly filled with two feather beds, twelve homemade sheets, twelve-grain sacks, two dozen face towels, and a number of tablecloths and scarves. The covering for the feather beds and all of the other items in my dowry chest were of linen that was made from flax that I had helped to plant, cure, spin and weave.

Relatives said that if I didn't marry before I was twenty, I might be an old maid that no one would want, but even that threat failed to put me in a marrying frame of mind.

In the absence of my father, Mother had been approached by several fathers and relatives of young men in the community about a marriage arrangement for me. A couple of times, Mother had been rather favorable, but I was unwilling. I didn't want to marry because, in my heart, was a dream—a dream of going to America.

So many off the men in our village had returned from America with wonders to relate of that far-away country. I dreamed day and night of going there and marriage to some boy I had known all my life had little attraction in comparison. So, when Mother mentioned the proposals to me, I said I wasn't ready to marry and she did not urge me further.

In this I was fortunate, because a girl usually had to marry the boy her parents chose for her.

Once or twice, I half fancied myself in love. The boys in the neighborhood with whom we had grown up and played as children often indicated their feelings long before there was a formal discussion of marriage by the parents. This was the case with Andre. Mother liked Andre and he pressed his suit with ardor.

One day, the hurdy-gurdy man and his wife came to Madarasul Mare. It was late when they stopped at our house and Mother invited them to spend the night. We brought in a great sheet full of straw and put it beside the stove, so they could sleep by the fire, and supplied them with extra cover.

We were sitting around the fire visiting when Andre came sloshing through the rain in his heavy boots. With all those people in the room he sat there and courted me. I was very much embarrassed.

The hurdy-gurdy man had a little blue parrot and a box filled with slips on which fortunes were printed. He would say to the parrot, "This young lady wants to know her fortune."

The fortune seeker would drop a few coins in the cup and the parrot would reach into the box and pull out a fortune. The next morning, the hurdy-gurdy man told my fortune.

His eyes twinkled as he said, "And the young man who came to see you last night is very sweet on you. I heard him talking, but you don't want him and I don't blame you. His nose is crooked just like my bird's nose."

Andre did have an odd looking nose and I was annoyed at his boldness of the night before. Our budding romance died.

Later, there was the miller's son, an educated boy who was more of a dreamer than a doer. But my dream of America was more real than love!

Dan's Disobedience Brought Me Luck

One morning in 1907, Mother and I walked to Satu Mare to market our cottage cheese, eggs, and onions. We had sold our produce and had started home when we saw six or eight men coming down the street with bags and bundles. They were happy and excited and were calling to people on the street. We paused to see what it was all about. And one of the men was Father!

None of the men had let their families know they were returning home because they wanted it to be a surprise. Father was so happy to see us and we to see him. He had brought home a small amount of money and right then and there, he gave Mother money to buy material to make me two suits. He couldn't get over the fact that I was a tall young lady.

Before we returned home, we bought some beautiful gray material and later I went to another village where I had a cousin who was a dressmaker. I stayed with her while she made my suits.

Father told us stories of America by the hour and it seemed I could never hear enough about it. My dream of going there became more consuming.

Several different men paid the ceremonial visit to my father to discuss my marriage to some village swain, but my stock answer was, "I'm not ready to get married."

How grateful I am that my parents neither urged nor commanded me to marry.

Shortly after Father returned home, my brother, Dan, also came back from America. He reached home in the middle of the night and surprised us. We had gone weaving earlier in the evening and had only been I bed for a short time. How glad we were to see him! We didn't do any more sleeping that night. Dan had gotten homesick, so he decided to come back with some other fellows for a visit.

But Dan wasn't happy in Romania. He talked constantly of America, where people could work and save money and get ahead. It was no surprise to any of us when he returned to America in less than a year. I wanted to go with him, but there was no money for a ticket.

After Dan went back to America, he took a step that greatly displeased my mother. He got married there without parental consent. It was a serious thing.

Romanian young people usually married right in their own village and were greatly influenced, if not absolutely governed, by their parents' wishes. Although he married a Romanian girl, Mother was very bitter about it.

"I will never forgive him," she said.

Dan was devoted to Mother and was anxious to get himself back in her good graces. So he wrote: "Mary has been wanting to come to the United States. If you are willing for her to come, I will send her money for the trip."

Mother said I might go. It seemed too good to be true!

I went outside and looked at the yellow stacks of hay, the familiar clusters of straw-thatched houses along the street, the great clods of dry earth along the well-worn paths. And then I looked at the deep blue of the sky with puffball clouds floating toward the Carpathians. I loved the land and I loved my people, but something seemed to be calling and calling to me from across the sea.

"Thank you, God," I whispered, "for making it possible for me to go to America."

Our street buzzed with excitement. All the old friends and my many relatives called to talk about the trip and to hear the progress of our plans. To my great joy, Julia, a friend who lived farther down the street, secured her parents' consent to go with me. How much more fun it was to plan our trip together! Of course, we would not make the journey alone, for each month anywhere from ten to twenty people from Madarasul Mare left for America.

The first step was to procure a passport. For this, a birth certificate was required, which we secured through the village priest. Next, we went to the city hall to have an application filled out to be sent to Caraeul Mare, a city considerably farther from home that Satu Mare. There we were told it would take two or three months to secure a passport.

Julia and I had hoped to leave with the January group, but when Father went to Caraeul Mare, the passport had not arrived. I had been particularly anxious to go with the January group because one man among the number who was returning to America, lived in Cleveland, Ohio, where I was to join my brother. Others planned to go to Illinois or elsewhere.

Another group was to leave on February 8, but Julia and I were still without passports. I wasn't yet seventeen, but I decided it would be better for me to see about the passport, as I spoke better Hungarian than Father, and the passport was secured from Hungarian authorities.

Julia, her mother and I walked the long miles to Caraeul Mare. There I talked with a young man who seemed to be in charge. I explained how we had waited anxiously for our passports and how we wanted to leave with a group of friends on the eighth of February.

He thumbed indifferently through a great stack of passports on a table and found ours almost at the bottom.

"We'll fix these up and sent them to you," he said.

"No, " I said earnestly. "I don't want to leave this office until I get my passport, and my friend here wants hers, too. If there are any charges, we will pay them. We don't want to miss that boat."

He grinned and said, "Alright."

We paid him a fee and he put our passports in order. Julia and I were in a joyful mood as we clutched these precious documents to us on our return home.

Now, we intensified our work of getting ready to go. Father gave me the large suitcase he had bought in America, so I didn't have to carry a reed basket or a huge, knobby bundle as so many of the immigrants did. I had my gray suit that Father had purchased for me when he returned from

America, and I had two good pairs of shoes. I felt that I looked very much like other people, as we who lived in Transylvania dressed like the Hungarian people, instead of wearing sectional peasant costumes.

All the unused space in my large suitcase was filled in with linens that I had woven myself. I had one other piece of baggage–a linen bag something like a shopping bag. It was filled with raw bacon, salami, and bread. My friends all said I should take some food along with me and I was very glad that I did.

Dan had sent me $100 American money, which was enough to buy my ticket. At that time, each $40 of American money was worth $100 Hungarian money;. When I was ready to go, Mother put another $40 in my hands.

"A girl in a strange country might need some extra money, Mary," she said. "I want you to have this."

I knew that my mother needed that $40, but I also knew that she wanted me to take it. "Thank you, Mother," I said. "I really might need it badly." My dear good mother, I thought. When I find work in America, I'll send this back to her and more.

We walked eight miles to take the train at Yidon, and many of our friends, both girls and boys, and many relatives came along with us. Since I was still a minor, one of the men of the party had signed my passport for me, and he was supposed to look after us. But by the time the train came, he was drunk.

My mother was deeply troubled. "Honey, you had better come back home and not go this time," she said. "That man is already drunk and I am afraid he won't behave. What will you do from here to America?"

I had a lot of confidence in my ability to look after myself. I didn't mean to be cruel to Mother, but having gone that for, I couldn't even think of turning back.

"No," I said positively. "I am going on and I will look out for myself. I am going if I have to swim part of the way!"

Finally, the train came and we boarded it. When I looked out on the friends and relatives who had come to the station to say goodbye and saw my mother crying, I seemed to crumple up inside. I sat down and covered my face and cried all night. But my determination to go to America did not weaken.

The next morning, we reached Budapest, Hungary, and from there, we took a train to Vienna. From Vienna, we took another train to Diume, which then belonged to Austria, and from there, we boarded our boat in pouring rain.

The boat was small and loaded with other peasants—Romanians, Poles, Hungarians, and Russians, who were following their dream of a better life in America. Some of the peasants, especially the middle-aged people, were terribly ragged and dirty, and I often saw lice crawling on their clothes.

First, we sailed on the Adriatic, then around the Italian boot to Naples, and then on out through the Straits of Gibraltar into the ocean. It took us twenty-one days to reach Ellis Island.

The food on the boat was terrible. We were supposed to go to the dining room for breakfast, lunch and dinner, but there was no variation in the menu of poorly cooked fish and macaroni. It made me sick to look at it even thought I proved to be a good sailor and didn't suffer from seasickness. We would get bread and coffee from the dining room and bring it back to our bunk to eat with raw bacon and salami. I first ate the bread I brought form home, but it was gone long before we reached America.

There was an Italian boy on the boat who had an accordion. He used to play on deck while the people danced. Julia and I had fun dancing up there, but a boy on the boat kept bothering us and making unwelcome advances. I asked him to behave, but he didn't, so one day, I became exasperated and slapped him. He said that he would have me sent back to Romania for acting as I did. I didn't really believe him, but his threat worried me. Julia and I stopped dancing and remained pretty much in our bunks.

Finally, we reached Ellis Island. First, we were all given a thorough physical examination by a doctor. Then we were each put into a corral, according to where we were going, and each had a number attached to his shoulder. We were supposed to stay in the corral until a man came along with a banner with which our number was printed. Then we were to follow him.

I was going to Cleveland, Ohio, and most of the rest of the party were going to Aurora, Illinois, so we were separated. I got out of my corral and ran back to say goodbye to my friends once more. A man grabbed me hard by the arm. I couldn't understand what he said, but he pointed to my corral, and wasn't at all gentle when he pushed me back into it. Plainly, I was to stay there.

After a while, a man come along and gave us our baggage, a piece of pie, a banana and a sandwich. I had never before seen a piece of pie, or a sandwich, or a banana. I ate the sandwich, along with some salami I had left and a piece of bread I had brought from the boat. When we were on the train, I offered the banana and the pie to a girl who took the food and seemed to enjoy it.

I reached Cleveland on Friday evening about eight o'clock, March 5, 1910, almost a month after I had left Romania. As I got off the train, I couldn't see my brother, but a man I had known at home was there, along with a friend of my brother.

The man with whom I was acquainted said, "Let's go. Your brother will find us later."

"I don't want to go anywhere until I see my brother," I replied. I sat down to wait for Dan, who came in a short time. It was wonderful to see him again!

We went to the corner and got on the first street car in which I had ever ridden. I looked around and saw the beautiful American women wearing hats and fine shoes and, suddenly, I was ashamed of the gray dress of which I had been so proud, and of my heavy shoes and my babushka. "Some day when my debts are paid, I'll dress like these Americans," I thought. "I'll be an American

So Different and So New!

When we reached my brother's house, I was introduced to my new sister in law. We had a happy time talking about the folks at home and what I could do in the new country. To me, their humble flat was truly magnificent. There was water right in the kitchen and a gas stove on which to cook. The beds had legs and were equipped with cotton mattresses. But, most wonderful of all, there was an inside toilet.

My sister-in-law had work in a tobacco factory and had to report for a half day's work on Saturday, so the first morning after my arrival, I was left alone. Everything was new and strange, and my sister-in-law didn't help matters any by cautioning me about so many things. She scared me to death.

She said, "Don't open the door, because some street bum might come in. Don't put up the shades because someone might look in and see that you are alone. Don't touch the gas stove because if you open the gas jet without lighting it, the gas will kill you."

All that morning, I sat in a chair and scarcely moved until my sister-in-law returned at one o'clock.

There was something that had puzzled me even before I left Romania. The man I had known in Madarasul Mare, who met me at the train in Cleveland, had written to his mother in Romanian that he was sending money for me to come to America. He said we would marry soon after I reached my brother's. When he was at the train, I wondered more than ever and I found he was boarding with my brother.

On Sunday, I got up the courage to ask who I owed for my ticket and told about the letter that had come to our village. My sister-in-law was very angry with this man for telling an untrue story.

"Anyone who would tell such a story is not a person I want to stay in my house," she said, and she made the man move that very day.

On Monday, my sister-in-law took me to work with her at the American Tobacco Factory on Ninety-Third Street in Cleveland.. I was to receive fifty cents a day for six weeks until I could learn to make cigars. How hard I worked to learn!

The leaves refused to stay in place for me and, after I had them neatly rolled, they had a habit of loosening up, until they looked like a long brown flower. At first, when no one was watching, I used to bite on the leaves to make them tender at the ends and more inclined to stay rolled. I wanted to learn to make good cigars, so I could pay my debts more quickly. It wasn't long before I could do good work and didn't have to resort to chewing the leaves to make them stay in place.

I felt very timid and shy those first days and, one day, while I was working in the factory, I suddenly sneezed so hard it startled the workers, and every machine on the floor of our factory stopped. I was so scared!

The foreman, half laughing, half scolding said, "Miss Szilagyi, if you are sick, you had better go to the hospital. We don't want you sneezing and stopping all the machines in the factory!"

On Wednesday evening, following my arrival in Cleveland, we washed our clothes in the kitchen and used a wash or rub board. I had never seen one and didn't know how to use it. Three boys had come to see me that evening and were in the kitchen talking and laughing as we worked. I didn't let on that I had never seen a washboard, and I scrubbed my knuckles more that I did the clothes. They were raw by the time we finished washing.

So many things impressed and interested me. There were automobiles, which I had never seen in Europe. There were streetcars on which we could ride for miles at little cost. There were the public buildings and department stores. The parks of the city were a perpetual wonder and delight. I thought Wade Park was the most beautiful place I had ever seen.

Once my brother and his wife took me on the roller coaster. I didn't know whether to hold to the seat or to my new American hat, of which I was so proud. After on big dip, I decided against the hat and clung to the seat.

Each Sunday, we went by streetcar to the West Side Church. It was necessary to transfer two or three times to reach there. We also went to dances on the West side. The Romanian people were a close-knit colony and I had little time for loneliness.

In those days, there were ten or fifteen Romanian boys in America to one girl. These boys had strict orders from home not to keep company with girls of other nationalities, so whenever a girl came over from Romania, there were a dozen boys eager to meet her, and to propose marriage if she was personable. I had had many beaux in Romania, but I had more in Cleveland..

The custom was for all of the boys to come Saturday or Sunday, or at any other time a girl was free from work. They would all stay and visit a while and then go, one by one. As each boy left the house, the girl was supposed to go outside with him and talk for a short time, so that the boy would have an opportunity to "speak his piece" privately. He usually tried to steal a kiss, too. It sometimes took a couple of hours to tell all the boys goodbye. However, if a girl became engaged, all the other boys would leave together and only the one to whom she was betrothed would remain.

Even though I had so many beaux, my thoughts kept going to the miller's son in Madarasul Mare who had tried to dissuade me from coming to America. We had been writing to each other for a while, when Mother found we were corresponding.

If I had married this boy in Romania, he would have had no objection, but she didn't think we should write to each other. She wrote me that I must stop writing him, and I obeyed her, although he still continued to write for a while.

At first, I concentrated on saving money, so that I could send Mother the $40 she had given me when I left there. I was also anxious to pay Dan the $100 he had sent me. I did not buy any new clothes or a pair of the American shoes I coveted. During Lent, I ate mostly bread and kept my food bill as low as possible. Before too many months went by, my debts were all paid, and then I greatly enjoyed buying some American clothes.

I was doing well at the tobacco factory. After I learned to roll cigars, I received $7 a week, which was good pay for a woman. But, in spite of earning good money, I wasn't entirely happy. Two things interfered with my happiness. First, my sister-in-law and I didn't get along together and, second I wasn't learning English.

I enjoyed working with the people I met at the factory and many of them were my good friends. However, they didn't speak English and many of them had no desire to learn it. They were mostly Hungarian, Polish and Syrian. I already spoke Hungarian and was learning to speak Polish, but I wanted to learn the language spoken by most of the people in this big, beautiful country that I loved more and more each day.

The trouble with my sister-in-law and me was that she, like practically everyone else I knew, thought I should get married, I was eighteen years old, and a girl couldn't just flit around and refuse her chances until she became an old maid. Then no one would want to marry her!

My sister-in-law, like most other Romanians, felt that the greatest happiness one could achieve would be to return to Romania with enough money to buy a large amount of land, thus becoming a power in the community. One man that she set her heart on my marrying was a landowner in Romania. She said we could work and save in America and go back and buy more land. I refused to consider it. The man was a drunkard and a bum. I would have been the one to work and save money!

In the meantime, I had been keeping company with another man that neither my brother nor my sister-in-law liked. Matters came to a climax between my sister-in-law and me, and I left my brother's home and my job at the factory, and worked for some wealthy people in Clifton Park as an "upstairs" girl. Another Romanian woman was the cook.

A little later, a young couple with a new baby hired me to do their housework. I did the cleaning, the cooking, and the ironing, but I lived elsewhere.

The first day, I worked hard to get everything done and in order. The young man brought in tow live pigeons and asked me to dress and cook them. He wanted pigeon soup. I got the birds on to cook and began the ironing.

The irons were a new kind to me. The handle hooked of for ironing and was removed when the iron heated. I didn't do a good job hooking the handle on and crash went the iron in the pigeon soup. I finished the iron out in a hurry before the man came to see what the noise was about.

"Something dropped, " I said without further explanation.

My next work experience in a home was with a very kind lady who had a large house and seven children, the youngest of whom was two years old. The children loved me and I learned English rapidly from them.

They would push me and say, "Mary, come give us bread. Mary, I want a drink. Mary, I want to go to the bathroom." Mary, I want to go and ride the pony."

And, in heeding their many demands, I learned English, which had been my chief reason for taking up domestic work.

In the meantime, my sister-in –law had written to my mother that I would not obey her or my brother.

I received a letter from Mother while my employer and her husband had gone on a trip to Niagara Falls. They had left me in charge of the big house, the seven children, a pony, and a pig. Mother's letter read:

Mary,

I have a letter from your sister-in-law that says you won't mind her or do what she tells you to do. If you can't get along with her, you had better come home. If you do not have any money to come on, I will send you some.

If you don't want to come home, go to Aurora, Illinois. A large colony of our people live there. Some of them from our own village. Don't stay where you are."

When my employer returned from Niagara, I read her my mother's letter. This lady had already asked me if I wouldn't like to go to school. I had said, "NO," because I just didn't know any better. In later years, I realized what a big mistake I had made by refusing.

When I read the lady my mother's letter, she said, "What are you going to do?"

"I will have to go to Aurora because I don't want to go back to Romania," I replied.

She said, "Oh, no, Mary. I hate to see you go to Aurora. It will be hard for you to find work there. You would be much better off to stay here with us."

I said, "I'm sorry, but I must mind my mother."

So I went to Aurora in July 1911. There, another letter from my mother awaited me.

She told me there were three boys living in Aurora that we knew and that I might marry one of them. Each of these boys had land in Romania. I could marry one of them and we could work for awhile, save our money, and return to Romania to tend the land.

One of the boys mother wrote about how he had already left for Europe. The other two were drunkards. The second boy went back to Europe and was killed in World War I. The third died in Aurora from drink.

I found Aurora was like my Cleveland employer had told me it would be. The cotton mill where most of the Romanian people found employment was closed down and numbers of people were without anything to do. Since I had had experience doing housework and had learned to speak some English, I found a job doing housework and was able to save some money.

I had Sunday off to go to church, and I also had Thursday afternoon and evening off. By that time, I had some beautiful clothes, most of which I kept at the home of a friend.

Among the many boys who came to see me in Aurora was one that I began to like more than any of the others. He was George Trippon, and I had known him as a child in Romania. Mother didn't favor George, not because she disliked him as a person, but because he had no parents and no land in Romania. She felt that if I married him, there would be no ties to bring us back to Romania.

Our young people observe St. Andrew's day when they are thinking of marriage and need guidance in making a wise choice. On that day, one eats nothing until evening. Throughout the day, whenever opportunity offers, one prays God to help him or her make a wise choice. Then, in the evening, the boy or girl takes a slice of bread and eats half of it. The other half is placed under the pillow. A glass of water is placed by the bed, but is left untouched.

The one observing St. Andrew's Day is supposed to dream of the future mate and, by that sign, knows whom to marry. If one doesn't get married that year, the fasting and prayer are repeated the next year.

I ate not breakfast of lunch that day and my employer kept asking, "Mary are you sick? Why don't you eat?"

I said, "I am not sick. I want to fast today."

When I finished the dishes, I went to my room and prayed until about nine o'clock. Then I put the glass of water on the stand by my bed and went to sleep. I waked very much puzzled, for I had dreamed of two men: the miller's son in Romania and George Trippon.

I dreamed that George was out in the field cutting hay and had a red handkerchief tied about his neck, but he left the field to bring me a glass of water.

It was after St. Andrew's day that Mother wrote me of a widower who was coming over from Romania. He had two children and he also had a considerable amount of land there. She wrote that she had made all the arrangements for me to marry this man..

That letter troubled me. I knew I didn't want to marry a widower I had never seen and take over the responsibility of his two children, land or no land. I wanted to marry George Trippon.

George's most frequent question had been, "When can we become engaged?"

So, the next time he came to see me, after I received Mother's letter, I said we would get engaged right away.

We told our news to the friend where I kept most of my clothes. She cooked a big ham, bought a couple of kegs of beer, a couple of bottles of whiskey, invited a number of people, and gave us an engagement party.

We had to wait three weeks while the banns were published at the church before we could be married on September 23, 1911. We had been married a week when the widower arrived from Romania.

George Trippon and a Boarding House for a Honeymoon

I had known George Trippon since my early childhood. He was born in the neighboring village of Rusi, where his family was well to do. His father was mayor of Rusi for sixteen years. George's mother died when her fifth child was born (the baby died too). There remained one older sister and three brothers. Two years later, his father died.

After his father's death, George stayed with his older brother's wife in Rusi while the brother was in the army. The sister-in-law was very unkind. She gave her small brother-in-law almost no food and, if she went away, she would lock him out of the house. Sometimes, he would be so hungry, he would climb in through the window and steal a slice of bread.

When he went to a home where the children had parents, he would stand close to the breadbasket, hoping that someone would give him food. One aunt his mother's sister, gave him food when she could.

When the brother came home from the army, the sister-in-law complained constantly about having to keep the boy. When George and his brother went to plough the land, George had to ride the plough horses and, instead of his brother telling him how to guide the animals left or right when they got out of line, the brother would throw a clod of dirt and hit George in the back.

They sent that seven-year old child to the woods for firewood once or twice a day. Finally the married sister, who lived right across the street from us in Madarasul Mare, came to Rusi on a visit. She learned how hungry her little brother was, how he had no shoes, and how often he had to go for firewood. She took him home with her and kept him with her until her was about ten years old. George played with us and we knew each other well.

One day when George was about ten, a man came to or village looking for a boy to herd his sheep. George worked for him for a couple of years. This man and his wife had no children and were very kind to their young helper.

At the age of twelve, George came back to our village and got a job taking care of a man's horses. He also worked in the field all day, came home for supper, took the horses to pasture, slept out there with them, and brought them back around four of five o'clock in the morning, to be ready to go to work in the field.

He came to America when he was seventeen. The brother, just older than he, was already in America and sent passage money. It was in 1907 that George joined his brother in East Chicago, Indiana. Times were hard and work was scarce. When they found work, the men often had to take their pay in script.

Temporary work at the steel mill played out and George, and another jobless fellow, went to Mendora, Illinois to look for work. Neither could speak English very well and they got lost. Finally, someone took them to the city hall where an employee could speak Romanian. This man advised them to go to Aurora, Illinois.

At Aurora, the railroad company hired them as section hands and sent them to Iola where they lived in bunk cars and did their own cooking. The section boss liked my husband and his friend so much that he told them to go back to Aurora and bring several more of their countrymen to work on the railroad. Later, George came back to Aurora to work in the railroad shops. He was employed there when we married.

When we decided to marry, I bought myself a beautiful bridal veil and a gown of white satin. We walked from my employer's house to the church to be married and I was so excited that I left my wedding ring at home.

In spite of my happiness in being married to George Trippon, there was a deep sadness in my heart on my wedding day because no member of my family was present to see me married. However, I had one consolation: Julia, the girl who was my companion on the journey to America, was with me. This did much to take away the sorrow of having no family present. When we reached America, Julia had gone directly to Aurora and married shortly thereafter. When I moved to Aurora, our friendship was renewed.

Julia was now expecting her first baby, but she and her husband stood for us, which is the Romanian way of saying she was matron of honor and her husband's best man. The expression " stood for" has a special significance. It implies a greater responsibility than Americans usually attach to it. It signifies the couple's willingness to be godfather and godmother to any children you may have, and should you die and leave children, the godparents will help them in every way possible.

From the church, we went to the Romanian hall for a wedding supper and dance.

The wedding supper started at five o'clock and was over around six-thirty. The tables were cleared from the hall and the dancing began.

At nine o'clock the Bride's Dance began. This is a modification of the old-country custom, and takes the place of the American custom of sending wedding gifts to the bride and groom.

In Europe, where the peasants are so poor, the Romanian bride never receives money from friends and relatives who attend her wedding. Her only gifts are homemade doughnuts to serve at the wedding dinner or eggs to make noodles. The people just don't have money to bestow presents.

In America, the best man officiates at the Bride's Dance. In the hall where the dancing takes place, there is a band stand and near it a large table. On the table will be a couple of dozen soup plates, nesting one inside the other, and two tin bowls into which the soup plates fit snugly. All of this is in preparation of the Bride's Dance.

When the best man calls out that the Bride's Dance is beginning, everyone forms a circle about the bride. There are usually from twelve to fifteen ushers at a wedding and, of course, other men are included in the circle. The head usher dances with the bride first and then other men come, one by one, to take the bride away from each successive partner.

Each one who claims her for a dance throws money on the table or at the soup plates. The best man manipulates the plates. When he puts a soup plate on top of the tin bowl and calls out, guests throw silver dollars and try to break the plate. During the course of the evening, the entire stack of soup plates will be broken.

The money thrown at the soup plates is given to the bride. Those who wish to give her larger amounts, pin checks or greenbacks on her dress or veil. When I married, I received about two hundred dollars. I had to dance three or four hours for it, and walk home a couple of miles after the dance was over.

Twenty-one years later, when my daughter, Emma, married during the depression, she received about six hundred dollars. But two hundred of that came from my husband and me. When times were good, a bride might receive from twenty-five hundred to three thousand dollars during the Bride's Dance. I was told that in one of the cities of Indiana, a girl married a man whose brother was mayor of the city and the Bride's Dance netted her fifteen thousand dollars.

Like many other Romanian weddings in those days, my wedding turned out to be a wild affair. The Luxembergers and the Romanians didn't get along and a few drinks under their belts put them in a fighting mood.

The younger brother of the man who signed my passport to come to America, had wanted to marry me. He got himself in fighting trim and started making trouble on the other side of the room. I was dancing with George when, all of a sudden, a bunch of people started fighting.

The priest went over to them and said, "You should be ashamed to make trouble here and embarrass this girl. She is from your own village in Romania."

But they didn't quiet down. My husband got in between the fighters and tried to stop them, but they got away from him, went outside and started to beat each other over the head. The police heard the commotion and came and took about thirteen of them to jail. No one could speak English well enough to explain what had happened.

The next morning, my husband went to the jail and bailed them all out. He had to pay five dollars bail for each one.

Sunday we were entertained by friends, but a portion of the day was spent negotiating the rental of a house and the purchase of its furnishings. When we married, I had paid my debt to my mother and brother and had saved $135 in addition. My husband had also saved some money.

We paid $150 for the boarding house furnishings and, of course, there was an additional monthly rental. The house had two rooms upstairs, and a large dormitory room and kitchen downstairs. My husband and I lived in one of the upstairs rooms and, in the other one, were three beds, which were occupied by six men.

In the dormitory room downstairs, we had enough double and single beds to accommodate twenty-four men. We had one single bed for a very old Serbian who read the Bible all day long. He had a trunk in which he kept his religious books and allowed no one to sit either on his trunk or his bed. He said that once, when he was younger, he fasted for forty days, but after five days, found he had to drink water.

I smile when I think of my "honeymoon" in comparison to the ones that many young people enjoy today. I married Saturday afternoon, danced miles for the money I received in the Bride's Dance, walked two miles back to the home of the friends where we spent the rest of the night, helped to negotiate the purchase of a boarding house on Sunday and, on Monday, began keeping borders.

Our arrangement for keeping these boarders was common enough then, but now it seems odd. I cooked for thirty men and also did their washing by hand. I was paid three dollars a month by each man for washing his clothes, furnishing him a bed in which to sleep, and cooking his breakfast and lunch, using the food with which he supplied me.

Each man paid for his own food, although I purchased it for him. Each had a special charge book from the grocer and paid this bill once a month.

As the man would leave for work, perhaps one would say, "I want a loaf of bread today, some tobacco, and a pound of pork chops."

Another might say, "I want liver, and cottage cheese, and potatoes."

I almost addled my brain trying to keep in mind who wanted what.

In addition to the breakfast-lunch preparation, I cooked the evening meal for everyone. My compensation for this was that I got my own food for this meal free of cost. I had a separate charge book from the grocer for the food for the evening meal and, at the end of the month, the expenses were divided among those who had eaten it. The cost of the evening meal usually came to $2.75 to $3.00 per person.

Some of the men used to grumble and say, "It looks like we had chicken every Sunday that we pay so high for an evening meal."

I got up at four o'clock in the morning, so I could fix coffee for the men and get everything in order for their breakfast and lunch. They didn't all work the same hours. Some had to leave the boarding house before six o'clock.

All day long, I prepared and cooked their different foods. I had little pans for each man and there was a cupboard with many drawers in it. When the food was ready, I would set each man's pans in the cupboard drawer in a specified place.

I prepared food in the Romanian way of cooking, as most of my boarders were Romanian. We had soup at every evening meal. I made all of my own noodles and rolled them out on a table with a broom handle for a rolling pin. The noodles were used in soup or became the basis for the men's favorite dessert, which was a mixture of noodles, cottage cheese, butter, salt, and sour cream with no sugar.

Most of the men fasted from cheese, meat and milk on Friday. So, I made them thin pancakes filled with mashed potatoes.

Once a week, I made rolled cabbage. I made raised doughnuts on Friday, and also another dish we called "Placinta," raised dough without eggs or milk in it. Placinta was filled with potatoes or sauerkraut and fried in a heavy skillet on top of the stove.

Our favorite Sunday dish was "chicken paprikash": chicken cooked with onions, celery and paprika . This meal was often finished off with rice pudding for desert.

In the middle of the dormitory room, we had a long table, reaching almost from end to end of the room, where the men sat to eat.

I washed twice a week. On Monday, I washed the men's underclothes and shirts, and on Thursday, I washed the bed sheets and towels. It was extremely dirty washing too, for most of the men worked in a foundry and came home as black as coal.

To keep everything running on schedule, I worked from fourteen to sixteen hours a day. I ran the boarding house for fourteen months while my husband worked in the railroad shops. During that time, my first child, Emma, was born with a midwife to look after me.

Emma came at two o'clock on a Friday morning. I stayed in bed Friday, Saturday and Sunday. On Monday, I cooked the evening meal for the boarders and, on Wednesday, with the help of my husband and one of the boarders, I washed. They did the rubbing and I rinsed the clothes and hung them out. By the time the last piece was on the line, I was so sick, I had to go to bed and George called the doctor. The doctor gave me some medicine and kept me in bed for a week.

I did my first machine sewing at the boarding house, as a sewing machine was included with the furnishings we had bought. I first mended sheets on it and, after Emma came, I made things for her. You couldn't buy ready-made dresses for babies then. When she was three months old, I made her first dress-a bright one!

Emma was no placid, cooing baby. She howled with the colic for six months and it was because I had such a time with her, that we sold the boarding house in 1913.

A Home and Reverses

When we sold the boarding house, we had saved enough money to make a down payment on a home. We watched the paper each day and, eventually, we saw a furnished house advertised that interested us. It had a good size basement, a large living room, a bedroom downstairs and two, upstairs. There was a coal range in the kitchen, a big round coal heater in the living room, a rug on the living room floor, and nice furniture throughout. And, best of all, there was a power washing machine! There was a big barn and an acre of land surrounding the house. We bought the place f or $1,900.

After buying our home, I kept from five to seven boarders, who slept in the bedroom upstairs. We put in a garden and cultivated the acre of ground. We had a couple of cows, a large bunch of chickens, and four pigs. Two of the pigs we butchered to keep and two, we sold.

After Mary, my second child was born, I didn't have time to keep boarders. Mary was born feet first. The midwife insisted she could get along without a doctor. After seventy-two hours of labor, I was having such a hard time that the midwife thought I was dying. She put me across the bed, grabbed the baby's feet and pulled her from me.

My baby's right arm was left crippled; her chin caught and the thyroid glands were injured. She never got over those birth injuries and would never be normal. But she is happy and well, and I have taken good care of her all these years.

On February 22, 1916, our son, George, was born on Washington's Birthday. How proud and happy we were and, of course, he could have no other name but "George."

Everything had been going along well and our house was almost paid for. Then my husband became ill with sciatic rheumatism and, for five years, was unable to work. He was a hot engine's mechanic and worked on the trains that were brought in. The engine room was very warm and the weather outside was cold and damp. We thought the continual changing back and forth caused his trouble.

We had a pretty hard time while George was sick, but I had a big garden and sold the extra produce. We had two cows and I sold and delivered milk. I also had eggs and chickens to sell. My husband had some type of insurance with the railroad company and, during the first year of his illness, he received $30 a month from it. The second year, he received $15 a month.

At the end of the third year, we were beginning to get behind with our grocery bill and the grocer was worried about it. I said, "Don't be afraid of us. We will pay." We were both brought up to believe that one is never free of an obligation until it is paid in full. We did pay every penny of the debt.

In spite of sickness and hard work, we had many happy times in our first home. We had our first Christmas tree there when Emma was two years old. That year she had her first doll and I hung it on the tree, along with Christmas tree decorations. Our good neighbors said my tree was lovely. We thought so, too.

We had comfortable beds and good food, and sufficient clothing. So many times I thanked God for all that we had and for the privilege of living in America.

During the time George was ill, he had different types of medical care, including baths at Hot Springs, Arkansas. The railroad gave us a pass and the children and I went with him.

Because of the two children, it was difficult for us to find a place to stay.

Finally, we found a house that belonged to a young man. He said we might move in if I would clean the house for him. I consented, although we still had to pay rent.

The streets in Hot Springs were narrow and the house we had rented was close against the mountain at the back. The front of the house was two stories high. I was busy cleaning and when I began to look for the children they were nowhere to be seen. I began imagining all kinds of things that might have happened to them; bears in the woods, a fall from the front of the house, and I ran frantically down the street.

There they were with their faces glued to the window of the newspaper office, watching the newspaper press.

A bad storm came while we were at Hot Springs. In Romania when a storm came, Mother used to have us kneel and pray until the storm subsided. Some vaudeville people lived in the front of the house and, each night, after their performance, they sang and jumped and practiced. To my distress, the storm made no difference in their routine. They went right ahead with their practicing while wind and thunder roared outside. According to the way I had been taught, this was very sinful, so I knelt and included them in the prayers I was offering for our own safety.

The baths did not seem to help George, so we decided to return to Aurora. I packed our clothes with the exception of the ones we were wearing and checked them on our ticket.

When we reached Aurora, I suggested, "Let's get our baggage and take a taxi home," but one of my husband's cousins who worked at the depot said he would bring the things to us on his truck. And then our baggage disappeared.

For several days, we didn't know what had happened to it, but later we found that the cousin had put the baggage on a truck with a company tag on it and someone took it over to the car shop. When we finally located our clothes, they were wet and beginning to mildew. Sweaters had faded on other clothing and many of our things were ruined. It was a real calamity.

George went to a Swedish masseur in Chicago who did help him considerably. It was while he was ill that George took out his first citizenship papers. He and one of his friends went to the city hall one day in 1914 and took out their first papers. I was so happy.

At that time and up until 1924, when a man who was the head of a family became a citizen, his entire family also became citizens. Yet things did not go as smoothly as we had expected. When George returned after two years for his second papers, he was told that a mistake in the place of residence had been made. Since we lived outside the city limits, he would have to start all over again. This made George angry and he dropped the matter. But it came up again when World War I began.

All aliens were called to the city hall to fill out papers and state whether or not they wanted to go into the army of the United States. When we went down to the city hall, George was still crippled with rheumatism and had to walk with a stick.

When asked if he would wish to join the army, he said, "I would go tomorrow if I could if you would take care of my wife and children."

The man with whom he was talking asked, "Then why didn't you take out your second papers? I see you made your first application."

Before George could answer, he was called to serve as an interpreter for someone, so I explained to the man what had happened with regard to George's application for citizenship.

Just then, the man who had refused George's second papers appeared in the doorway and I said, "There is the man who wouldn't give my husband his second papers."

The two men talked together and then our interviewer returned and said, "If Mr. Trippon will come back to the city hall right away, we will give him his second papers."

My husband worked hard to learn everything he could about the history and government of our adopted country, and Mr. Philip Jungles was his character witness when he received his citizenship papers. We were both so proud to be citizens.

There was a wonderful woman in Aurora, Mrs. Richard Curry, who did so much for the Romanian and Hungarian women of our city. She taught them English and maintained classes to help them learn how to take out their citizenship papers. I very deeply appreciated the work she did among our people and we became good friends.

My fourth and last child, Florence, was born October 14, 1918 and was named after my husband's sister. She arrived in the midst of the flu epidemic that took so many lives that year. At the time, I had three boarders: my younger brother whom Dan had sent for and two cousins.

With a tiny baby, three other children, four men, two cows, several pigs, and a large flock of chickens to look after, I had plenty to do. Then George came down with the flu. He was taken to the hospital a very sick man. For a time, I panicked completely.

When my good neighbor came in, she found me crying and wringing my hands. "What will I do with the children and the animals if I get sick, too?" I sobbed.

The church bells were tolling the death knell over and over for the victims of that dreadful influenza.

My friend, Abbey, said calmly, "Well, you just can't get sick."

She came with a quart of whiskey and put me and the four children to bed. She put the whiskey bottle by my bed and said, "If you feel yourself getting a chill, take just a little of the whiskey."

Then she called Dr. Kitenplom, our kind good doctor who was our friend through the years. Dr. Kitenplom said he couldn't come right away, as he had seventeen calls ahead of me, but he would come when he could.

I was sound asleep by the time he reached our house. He wakened me and examined me carefully and then he looked at each of the children. "You are not sick," he said. "You are just scared. What you need, my dear girl is courage. You can't allow yourself to become sick with worry. That won't help your husband or your children. You must think of them."

Dr. Kitenplom's lecture gave me strength to face up to the tasks that lay before me.

George went to the hospital on Friday, and, on Saturday I got someone to stay with the children while I went to visit him. When I reached his bedside, I found him on the verge of pneumonia and he hardly knew me. I said to the head Sister, "I just can't let my husband die. What would I do with my little ones at home?"

The Sisters who were desperately weary from their work in an over-crowded hospital rallied to my plea. They gave George special treatment and the next time I went to see him, he was much better.

When Easter came, I took eggs, sour cream and cottage cheese to the Sisters to show appreciation for their goodness to my husband.

We were so much more fortunate than many others. My friend, Julia, who had come over with me from Romania was one of the unfortunate. Her husband, a young brother who had just arrived from Europe, and her three children were all down with it at one time. First, her husband and then her young brother died. Poor Julia was heartbroken and bereft.

She never married again, but got a job in the railroad shops to support herself and her children.

After George came home from the hospital and was feeling better, he decided to go back to work, but he was too crippled to walk to the shop. A neighbor had a horse and an old wagon that had no regular seat in it. He said we might use this transportation. I was afraid of the horse, because in Europe I had worked only with oxen, but I took George to work each morning.

One morning, the horse got scared and started to run. We had just turned to cross the streetcar tracks on the main street and the wheel of the wagon caught in the rail track. I had a quart of milk in my hands and when the wheel caught, the nails in the makeshift seat came loose. I fell and smashed my mouth and knees against the pavement and sprained my right wrist. George was knocked unconscious.

Half dazed, I jumped up and ran the whole block trying to catch the horse. Someone else caught him and led him back to the scene of the accident. My husband was still lying there unable to move. A kind lady took me into her home and put iodine on my cuts and bruises. The people re-hitched the horse to the wagon, put us back into it, and told us to go home. When we got there, we couldn't get out of the wagon. The neighbor women came and carried us in, put us to bed and called Dr. Kitenplom.

In a few weeks, when he recovered, George again tried to go back to work. The shop foreman was considerate and gave my husband the lightest tasks, but he just wasn't able to work. My brother, Dan, who still lived in Cleveland, Ohio, heard of our trouble and wrote us that he now had his own business. He said we could work for him. After thinking it over, we decided to sell our house and livestock, and move to Cleveland.

When we reached Cleveland, my brother met us and took us to his home, and soon my children went out to play with his children in the backyard. He and my husband went to get beds for us. They left the gate open and Mary, who was then about six years old, left the other children and tried to follow the wagon. No one missed her for a long time and then she just couldn't be found.

My sister-in-law ran over to the drug store and called the police who said a lady had picked up a little girl about twenty blocks from there. The drugstore proprietor had a car and he and my sister-in-law went after Mary and brought her home. They put her in the backyard and closed the gate. Mary walked backwards and fell down the basement steps and cut her head so badly that we had to rush her to the dispensary to have her head sewed up. That was truly "Mary's Day," and it seemed that the days that followed were almost like it in the various mishaps that befell us. We were homesick for Aurora, and most particularly for the house we had sold.

We only stayed three months in Cleveland. Then we returned to Aurora. When we had left there, the sale of our house, furniture and livestock had brought us $2,800. When we moved back three months later, we only had $2,200. A loss of $600 in those days would be the equivalent of almost ten times that much now.

The people who had bought our home would not sell it back to us and we couldn't find a house to rent because of our four children. We lived with my husband's brother for a month, but we each had four children, and that was too large a family! Finally, we found a house we could rent. My husband got work with Richard Wilcox, a firm where machinery is made, but he couldn't hold the job because of his hip trouble. He was still bent over and unable to walk straight.

Finally, I said, "There is only one thing left for us to do. You stay home and look after the children and I will find work."

At that time, a few women worked in the railroad car shops, so I went to the C.B.&Q. Railroad shops and said to the boss, an Irishman by the name of O'Neill, "Mr. O'Neill, I want a job."

He said, "We don't need any more women. We have all we can handle now."

"My husband worked here for eleven years," I replied . "And the work he did caused his sickness. Perhaps, if I go to the brick office and talk with the big boss, he will find me something to do. I need work."

Rather than permit me to go elsewhere, Mr. O'Neill said, "Come back tomorrow ready to work."

My job was in the department where the men worked on railroad cars. They would drop nails and screws on the ground while they were working. Several women, I among them, picked up the nails and screws, took them to a large bench and sorted them into containers for the men to use again.

A Toehold on Pigeon Hill

After I had been working at the shops for a while, my husband's brother heard of a little cigar and grocery store that was for sale. We went to see the proprietor and found he didn't own the building but leased it for $25 a month. He wanted to sell us his stock and fixtures for $3,000. We said we would think it over and asked who owned the building, so that in case we decided to buy his stock and fixtures, we could be sure of continuing the store's lease. He gave us the owner's name.

When we went to see the owner, he said, "Why don't you buy the building instead of the fixtures! I will sell it for $3,500.00."

The building was twenty by fifty feet, but there was a partition at the back to make a pool room. The part used for a store was twenty by thirty feet.

I thought to myself, "We could live in this back room until we could do better, and have our store at the front."

We decided to buy the building.

The owner of the stock and fixtures was very angry when he heard of our decision, so angry that he damaged the building by knocking off the door knob and breaking glass. Then he called us to come and make repairs.

"You are the new owners," he said, "so you have to fix things and keep the place up."

He and his customers poked fun at us. "What are you going to do with a sick husband and four children?" he asked. "Where are you going to live?"

"We are going to live in the room at the back and have the store in the front," I said.

"Why don't you put the store in the back and live in the front? You would have just as many customers," he jibed. "You won't have any business anyway. You don't know anything about how to run a business."

"No," I said. "But we will learn."

At that time, there was bitterness on the part of the Germans and Luxembergers toward the Romanians and Hungarians. They called us "Hunkies."

The proprietor said to his friends, "I'll make those Hunkies come to me on their knees and ask me to take the store over again. They won't be able to run it. I am going to buy more and more stock and sell to everyone in the neighborhood. I'll sell cigars and cigarettes by the case, so there will be no need to buy from the Hunkies."

We were deeply troubled by his reaction against us and grateful, indeed, to a man who came to our defense-the Luxemberger from whom we had bought groceries and who had once worried because we owed him $80.

He said to many people, "The Trippons are good people. They are worthy of your help and support. They were my customers for seven years, and they are honest and square-dealing. I would buy all of my groceries from them if I didn't have a grocery store of my own."

When we finally opened up our business, our Luxemberg friend used to stop and buy cigars and newspapers, and pass the time of day. His friendship meant a great deal to us.

The man from whom we bought the building was also friendly and helpful. We told him the trouble we were having with the original lessee of the building. He said the man's lease would expire on the twenty-second of December.

"Come with me to my lawyer," he said, "and I will have him write this man that he is to get out when his lease is up."

It was surprising what a friendly feeling that notice seemed to awaken in the man! He came over to us one cold, snowy evening. I had just returned from the railroad shop. He pounded on the door and asked to come in, and he was so friendly!

After a while he said, "Please don't put me out on the twenty-second of December. If you do, I will miss the business of the two Christmases and New Year's."

Now, although the Russian Orthodox church still follows the Gregorian calendar, the Romanians follow the American calendar, but in those days the Romanians were still celebrating Christmas and New Year according to the Eastern calendar: Christmas on January 7th and New Year's on January 16, and then, of course, there would also be Christmas and New Year's according to the American calendar. If he left on December twenty-second, he would miss the business of these four big holidays. As a concession, he said that if we would let him stay, he would sell us the ice cream counter, the gum, candy, and cigar cases, and the ice box for $500! If not, he would have to remove those fixtures. We told him we would think it over.

The next day, I went to work and my husband went over to the store to talk further with the proprietor. Before he left the store, George had signed a paper agreeing to let the man stay until the middle of January and for us to buy $500 worth of fixtures and stock. There was a verbal agreement that we could choose any kind of stock we wanted, but when the time came for choosing, the man had sold all the goods of any value and had left us a lot of dried up shoe polish and other stuff we could not sell. He was also telling the neighborhood that he would make us like what he had done and that, in three months, we would be coming back to him on our knees. I think he probably underestimated the strength of our knees.

It was true, however, we had no money to buy stock, for we had put everything we had into the building. Almost from the time he had come to America, my husband had put money into the Aurora Building and Loan Association. From this firm we had borrowed money to finish paying for the building, a loan we paid back at the rate of $15 a month for eleven years.

One morning, while we were getting ready to open the store, we heard the bells tolling. First a big bell tolled and then two smaller bells, which is the way a death is announce. Then our next-door neighbor brought the word that one of our cousins had died.

This cousin had helped us so much after George became ill. He was the one to whom we could always turn for help. He was handy with tools and we had counted on him to help us fix up the store. Now, after an illness of a few days, he was dead from an infected tooth. Our main source of unfailing help and sympathy was gone.

We moved into the back of our store late in January. We asked friends, many of whom we had helped in the past, for a loan of $500, so we could buy stock. They refused, because they were afraid we would never be able to pay them back. Finally, one of my cousins by the name of Louis Ranke came to see us.

"You don't have any stock for your store," he said.

Louis let us have $500 with which we bought a stock.

The proprietor had sold his cigar license to another fellow and left us without one. His license would expire in April and a new one cost $75, which we did not have. Again, we had to try to borrow. A friend of mine had nine children and I had stood as godmother for all of them. We explained our need to her, saying we were afraid to sell tobacco without a license, as we might get into trouble. She let us have the $75 for the new license.

Then our real struggle began. It seemed, at first, that all the people who came in wanted something we did not have. George would get on the streetcar and go out and buy a half dozen of this and that. We were fortunate that two wholesale tobacco houses trusted us with cigars and cigarettes. As we sold, we paid them.

Every night when I took the money from the cash register, I prayed God to help us succeed and not let us lose everything we had worked for. Many of our friends said we would be better off to go back to Europe, but neither my husband nor I wanted to go back there to live.

While things were at their worst, our baby, Florence, became ill. I called the doctor, who said she had measles and he would have to quarantine us. I was terribly distressed because we were living in the back of the store and, I knew if there was a quarantine sign at the front that we would lose even the few customers we had.

I said "Oh, Doctor, our business is so bad. If you put a quarantine sign on the door no one will come in."

"I am sorry," he replied, "but I can do nothing else. I must report to the Health Officer. I'll ask him to put the sign on the back door, and just don't let the children come in."

The Health Officer sent a man that afternoon to put up the sign. But that night a big wind came and did us a good turn. It blew the sign completely away and no one ever returned to put up another. I used every precaution and, I am sure, no one caught measles from our household.

We still needed more working capital, so I went to Chicago to see my brother, George, who had a good job. He let us have $250 and said he would help us further if we needed it. We limped along until Spring. Then, business began to be better. Ice cream was our salvation. We sold a lot of it and, as we took in more money, we bought more stock.

My husband was still suffering with sciatic rheumatism, but he helped all he could, especially with the ice cream. Sometimes, he would work until he fell because his leg was so bad. On more than one occasion, a couple of customers would pick him up and carry him into the back room and put him to bed. However, after we had been in business for about a year, George's health began to improve. When we opened the store, although he is six feet tall, he weighed only 130 pounds. Twelve years later when we left Aurora to come to California, he weighed 240 pounds.

I opened the store at five o'clock in the morning and we kept open as long as there was any business. Often we closed at one o'clock in the morning. For years, we worked more than eighteen hours a day.

Business gradually became good and we paid off all our debts. Then we built on two bedrooms, a living room and kitchen to the store.

Our daughter, Emma, was a wonderful help. She was only eight years old when we opened the business, but she started to work right away, and could soon wait on a customer as well as anyone. She wasn't tall enough to see the scales, so my husband made her a little bench to stand on.

From the beginning, we tried to make ourselves a part of the community. Our store was always a voting center when city and state elections were held. I learned as much as I could about voting procedures and always tried to help others, especially the Romanian women.

Our precinct was known as the Pigeon Hill precinct and from 1200 to 1500 votes would be cast there. It was the largest precinct in the city and it was said that whichever way the Pigeon Hill vote went, the election would go. Although we never plunged into politics, we were always very much interested in the election and used to stay up for the returns until two or three o'clock in the morning.

Since we had our citizenship papers, my husband and I were witnesses for many of our countrymen who were applying for citizenship. Each applicant had to have two witnesses that had known him for at least five years. We encouraged friends to work to become American citizens.

At that time, a majority of the Romanians could not speak English and were treated like strangers. Today there is a change. The children of that older generation all speak English and America is their land. Many of them take part in the city government and some hold public office.

Another way in which we made ourselves a part of the community was through our telephone. At that time, there were only a few telephones in the neighborhood and, whenever an emergency arose, day or night, people came to our place to telephone. We lived back of the store and were, therefore, available.

After our business was launched, we never again had such a struggle. Of course, there are always high and low points. There was, for example, the day the Gypsies came; the caravan type who steal anything. Two men and three women came in the store and asked whether we spoke Romanian, Hungarian or English.

One of the women said to my husband, "Let me touch and count your money. If I count it, you will have good luck."

Another one asked me to sell her some ribbon.

I was sure that they wanted to steal from us and said, "You people had better get out of here. If not, I will call the police."

They ran out to their car and drove away. But the woman had touched our money!

We were told in Romania that evil would come of money that Gypsies put their hands on. All that I had been told and believe as a child came over me. I was afraid of evil spirits and that the money might disappear. I didn't want to leave it in the cash register, so I put it in a sack and took it to the bank right away.

One evening, when I was alone, I heard noises in the basement and decided someone was stealing the surplus goods we kept there. I barricaded the door and called the police. Two policemen came and went down the stairs.

They opened the door and called, "Come out of there!" And out jumped four or five big rats!

The men laughed and said, "See, Mrs. Trippon, there are your burglars!"

Our city, like others in the area, had trouble with Al Capone's gang. One evening I thought my husband had gone over to the Romanian hall. I heard sirens and a great commotion and then I heard on the radio that gangsters had robbed the people in the basement of the Romanian hall.

George often had several hundred dollars in his pocket at the close of the day. I just knew he was one of the victims.

A plain-clothes officer in the basement had shot one of the gangsters and had himself received a leg wound. Another man had also been wounded.

I had worked myself up into a major tizzy when in came George. He'd been visiting with a neighbor across the street and knew nothing of the hold-up at the hall.

Our children had their share of accidents. Mary was struck by a car. She grabbed the bumper and was dragged about a hundred feet. She got a pretty bad cut on the head, but the injury was not critical. Our son, George, was less fortunate.

When he was about seven, he ran out into the street after a ball and was struck by a car. His right leg was broken and, when I picked him up, I could see the bone sticking out through the skin.

Dr. Kittenplom took him to the hospital, operated on him and fastened a steel brace to the bone. After ten weeks, George came home from the hospital, but he had to go back again for or more surgery. The last operation enabled him to walk without a limp.

As in Romania, our social life centered about church activities and our Romanian hall, where dances and other social functions were held. Most of the Romanian boys and girls worked in the cotton mill, and our priest always asked the manager to let them have a three-day holiday at Easter, at Pentecost, and at Christmas, and his requests ware always granted.

It was during this period, that I taught myself to read English and the street car signs were my teachers! I learned to read by interpreting words from the pictures on the signs and it was always interesting to see how much of a new sign I could make out when it was first placed in the streetcar. Next, I learned to read and enjoy the newspapers; a habit I still have.

When my children were small, I sent them to the priest to learn to read and write Romanian. Their knowledge of Romanian has been a great help and satisfaction through the years, as we kept up a correspondence with relatives in Romania until the Iron Curtain descended. Also, when the members of the family were separated, I wrote the children in Romanian and they answered me in English.

From the time George began school, his teachers would tell me he had an unusual talent in art. We had hoped he would go to college and be a doctor or a lawyer, but his interests were not in those fields. He liked to dance and to dress people up. Other children would come over to play and I would hunt up everything I could find, so they could play "dress up." I even gave them my wedding dress to play in. George was in his glory when he assisted them in their costuming. He would add a bow here and a streamer there, and achieved some surprising effects. I really think his play experience had something to do with his becoming a designer of women's clothes.

As soon as our business was doing well enough to justify it, I took George and Florence to a good dancing school.

Return of the Native

Early in 1927, 1 heard the exciting news that our priest in Aurora would head a party of Romanians on a trip back to Romania. My mother had died in August 1922, but my father was still living, and I had aunts and many cousins living in Madarasul Mare. For several days, I could hardly sleep, thinking how wonderful it would be if I could go with this group to Romania. When I mentioned it to my husband, he was willing for me to go. He would have liked to go, too, but we couldn't both leave the store.

I went to Chicago to secure my passport and had to pay a visit to each of the French, Swiss, Austrian, Hungarian and Romanian consuls. To each, I paid $5 for a visa, except to the Romanian counsel, whose charge was $10. My third class roundtrip ticket cost $198, and we sailed on a large English Boat, the Aquitania.

There were ten men in our party, including the priest, and three women. One of the women with me was a cousin, the other a friend who lived in Aurora.

How very different things were from when I came to America on that shaky little boat seventeen and a half years before! The Aquitania was like a big hotel, and even third class travel was comfortable.

It was a beautiful water voyage and I was a good sailor. However, my cousin was very seasick. Seeing her so sick made me feel a little squeamish, and I thought we would be better in different quarters. I went to the steward and asked if we might move higher up. He said he had no more rooms up there.

"I remember now, Madam, I do have one berth, but it is close to the elevator and it will be very warm."

"I like it warm," I said.

So we moved to a more comfortable berth.

Within five days after we set sail, we reached Cherbourg, France. From Cherbourg, we took the train to Paris. Our main sight-seeing in Paris was to be when we returned, but soon after we arrived at the hotel, I suggested to my women companions, "Let's walk around and see what we can see."

As we walked down the street, we saw a bakery and decided to buy something to eat. A young girl came to wait on us. We selected some cream rolls and apple tarts, but she had no bag to put the food in. We were supposed to have brought a basket. When I offered her an American dollar in payment, she shook her head, showed us the door and took everything we had bought from us. We didn't understand her actions, but we heard later that some of the small storekeepers had been fooled by American soldiers who had sometimes "paid" in coupons and pieces of paper that were not money. Consequently, American tourists were not trusted, and it was only in large establishments, where employees were familiar with money exchange, that American money would be accepted.

We went to one of the large restaurants and, after considerable palaver, secured a handful of coins in exchange for American money. We returned to the bakery and held out our French coins. The girl took some of them and gave us the tarts and cream rolls that we coveted.

From Paris, we took a train to Romania. It was June and summer in the valleys and winter in the mountains. We could see the shepherds coming down from the mountains in their sheepskin coats and mufflers about their ears. From the mountain slopes, we looked down on high steepled churches and stretches of orchards, and, as the train wound in and out through the many tunnels, we saw the cattle on the slopes and, all over the countryside, the people going about their daily business of living. Many times we would see funeral processions or wedding processions.

An amusing incident occurred on the train. A man boarded the train in Switzerland who had been up in the snow. He spoke German, which I do not speak, but he talked quite a bit with one of the men in our party who spoke his language.

Finally, the Romanian with whom the man from the snows had been conversing came to me with a twinkle in his eye and said, "The man I've been talking with has asked me to say he'd like for you to change your plans and go to Germany with him."

I said, "Tell him, please, I couldn't do that. I have a husband and four children at home. They are expecting me back."

Presently, the Romanian returned and said, "Well, if you can't marry him and go to Germany, he would like to exchange coins with you."

I laughed and said, "I can do that." I gave him an American dime and he gave me a German coin to add to my collection.

In beautiful Vienna, where we had a stop-over, we saw Emperor Frances Joseph's palace and gardens.

During World War I, our priest had been with the Romanian soldiers and had accompanied them from Romania to Vienna and on to Paris. He told us there was bad feeling among the Yugoslavs, the Hungarians, and the Romanians, and while we were in Hungary, it would be better not to tell anyone that we were Romanian. As our train moved along, he pointed out to us the different spots where battles had taken place during the war.

As we passed the boundary of Austria, we came to a city by the name of Garge Var. It was there that I had the first indication of how the Hungarians felt about the Romanians. A very attractive looking lady boarded the train with her fifteen-year-old daughter. Everyone knew we were Americans by our clothes, shoes and suitcases. The lady visited with us and was very pleasant. She was the wife of the mayor of Garge Var and was on her way to Budapest.

She remarked, "Budapest, you know, is really two cities in one. The one towards the west is Buda, and the one towards the east is Pest."

Before we parted she asked where I was going. When I said, "To Satu Mare," she remarked, "I am sorry you have to go there. They are not our people in Satu Mare. They are all those dirty Romanians."

I only said, "Well, my people are there and I have to go where they are."

When we reached the depot in Budapest we had to register with the officials. Some of our group went on because they could not afford to wait for a better train, but six of our party stayed at a hotel across from the depot.

One of the ladies in our group decided to wash her hair while she was at the hotel. When we went to check out the next morning, the hotel keeper claimed that in washing her hair she had stopped up the plumbing and our bill was about $50 American money, which was supposed to include the cost of unstopping the plumbing. It was highway robbery, but there was nothing we could do but pay it.

We left Budapest that morning and the train stopped in Dobricin for lunch. As we went toward the restaurant, we saw a group of Hungarian peasants on their way to chop' wood in the forest. They saw the car we were on and knew it was going to Romania. They began swearing at us and at the train. We went on into the restaurant and ate, but we kept together.

As we returned to the train, one of the men made a mistake and got on the train that was returning to Budapest. We waved and called to him and he looked out of the window and saw us. He jumped off the train he had boarded and hurried over to get on with us. At the next station, two gendarmes were waiting for or him. They took him in the station and made him pay a fine for getting on the wrong train.

When we reached the Romanian border, we remained in the same car, but it was switched to a train that awaited it on the Romanian side. I listened to the Hungarian conductor as he gave instructions to the conductor on the Romanian train. He called attention to the good condition of the car and said he wanted it to be in the same condition when it was brought back to Hungary.

One of the first things that struck me was the apparent poverty of the Romanian railroad. Our conductor wore peasant clothes and a conductor's cap. I was told later that the railroad employees were paid so little for their work that they were unable to buy uniforms.

Shortly after we entered Romania, the train halted and an inspector boarded it. Four soldiers, with their guns and bayonets, accompanied him. They started at once to open up the suitcases and turned everything inside out. I had muslin and some other material in my suitcase.

The inspector said, "Madame, you can't take this material into Romania. You can only take ready-made clothes."

I said, "Look! I don't want to take anything out of Romania. I came to bring things to my family. How would it be if I gave you a couple of American dollars?"

Right away, he said to the soldiers, "Pack that bag up and close it."

He permitted the rest of our party to do the same thing, and let us go by with all that we had. However, we had to fill out a paper telling how much money we had with us, how long we planned to stay, and how much money we expected to leave with.

On the boat, we had changed a considerable portion of our American money into Romanian money. Our priest advised us to do this, as we were taking money entrusted to us by Romanians in Aurora to their relatives and friends. He thought we should have the correct amount to give each person, as we might not be able to make the exchange when we arrived.

My ticket read to Satu Mare, but I remembered that a first cousin lived in a village nearer to my own, so I got off there. As I left the train, I met a man I had known when he was a boy. I asked him where my people lived in the village. He told me, but said that they were all in the field at work. It was harvest season during which the people work from about four o'clock in the morning until ten o'clock at night.

I stayed in the village and talked with a great many people until my relatives returned from the field. They hitched their two horses to their wagon and took me to my old home at Madarasul Mare. It was one o'clock in the morning when we reached there. My sister knew I was enroute, but didn't know when I would arrive, so everyone was sound asleep.

I pounded and pounded on the door, but no one came. People seldom lock their doors in Romania, so I opened the door and called, "Julia! Julia! Wake up and put on the light. It is Mary from America!"

Finally, my brother-in-law got up and lighted the kerosene lamp that hung from the rafters. He was so excited that he struck three matches before he could light the lamp. By that time, the whole neighborhood was there. We were all so glad to see each other that we didn't go to bed until four o'clock in the morning.

It was hard for me to realize that the young woman who was the mother of two children was my little sister, Julia. She was only eleven years old when I had left home seventeen and a half years before.

My stay at the old home was saddened because my mother was no longer there. She had been dead almost five years. Although my people had written me of her death, I now heard the details. It seemed that her early death was such a waste of a useful life. If she had had the proper medical care, she might have lived many years. For Mother died at age forty-five.

It was Stork Day in August when she went out to milk a wild, nervous cow. Mother usually tied the cow's front feet to the feeding trough before milking, but this morning, she was in a hurry to get through and go to church, and neglected the precaution. The cow kicked her and then stepped on her bare foot. The injury was very painful and Mother stayed at home all day in bed. There was no doctor in the village and she didn't seek one elsewhere. Instead, she went to work in the field the next morning. Then, when it began to rain, she went with a group to pick mushrooms in the woods. While there, she scratched the top of her foot where it was bruised and swollen. Then, the next day, she went back to work in the field. She worked until she could go no longer. Father made a bed of straw in the oxcart and covered it with a homemade sheet, so that she could lie down on her way to the doctor.

The doctor took one look at her foot and leg and said, "Take her to Satu Mare to the hospital. She is going to have to have an operation."

Mother was in the hospital for a couple of days and, on the second day, she heard the doctor and a nurse talking. They said they were going to remove her leg above the knee. She was on the second floor of the hospital, but after the doctor and nurse went away, she got out of bed and managed to get to a window.

She looked out and saw a Gypsy woman going by. Mother called and asked the Gypsy to go to Madarasul Mare, find my father and tell him to come with the cart and take her home.

"Tell him," she said, "they plan to cut off my leg, and I do not want to be crippled. Tell him if he doesn't come for me, I will jump out the window. I won't stay here for them to operate on me.

The Gypsy woman went to our village and the very first person she met was my aunt's daughter. The Gypsy said, "I am looking for Peter Szilagyi. I have a message for him from his wife."

My cousin took the Gypsy to my father and he brought Mother home that day. The poison from her leg spread all over her body and, at the end of three weeks, she died.

Two things influenced my mother in her determination to come home to die. She did not want to live and be a cripple. She could not have purchased an artificial limb, and would have been unable to carry on as she had done before.

She probably felt that her time to die had come and wanted to be buried in her own village. The old superstition that if a corpse were brought across the farm lands, destruction of the crops would result, would prevent burial in her own village. My mother's love for her own land and her own village was one of the strongest emotions of her life.

Before my mother died, she left a will disposing of the twenty-four acres of land she had inherited from her father. In Romania, there doesn't have to be a written will, if there are the proper witnesses. My mother said:

"I have two sons and two daughters. Both of my sons are in America. To my daughter, Julia, who is here with me, I leave twelve acres of land and the house, with the understanding that she will take care of my husband as long as he lives in the house. To my daughter, Mary, I leave the other twelve acres. Mary is in America, but I have always loved her and wanted her to come back home."

My father was not living with my sister, Julia, but had remarried and lived with his wife, a kindly, middle-aged woman, only a short distance away. I was told that my brother-in-law had treated my father badly; that he had even beaten him.

I said to my sister, "Why did you let your husband beat my father?"

She said, "I couldn't help it. If I should tell him not to beat Father, he would beat me, too."

One of the conditions of my mother's will was that my brother-in-law and sister were to work the twelve acres of land that were mine and give the proceeds from the crop to my father.

One day Julia said, "Mary, would you come to the city hall with me and give me the little piece of paper that says I may have your twelve acres of land?"

"I didn't come here for the twelve acres of land," I replied. "I came to see you and Father, and the other relatives and friends that I love. It is a great sorrow to me that I can't have a visit with Mother, but I can respect her wishes. I would never give you any paper that would change the way Mother left her will, until after Father dies. Then you may have the land. I don't want it."

While I was visiting in Madarasul Mare, I spent most of my time with Julia, but one day, Father asked me to spend the day with him and his wife. They wanted to cook a duck for me. When we reached his house, my step-mother had gone to the woods to get fuel with which to cook. Soon she came with wood on her back, just as we used to carry it. Father cut the wood and started a fire, using straw and sunflower stalks as kindling. He took the big hand broom made of willows with which he swept the yard, pressed it down on the duck's head and caught her. We had a meal of duck soup.

It was dark by the time I was ready to return to Julia's, and Father walked home with me. There were no lights in the street. The only light came from the windows of the houses, as people have no curtains or shades over the windows. People always go to bed in the dark so no one can see them undressing.

It was almost two weeks before I had a chance to visit Mother's grave. The folks had been so busy with the harvest that they had not had time to show me where she was buried. But one morning, about four o'clock, Father came by and said, "Get up and dress. I will take you to the cemetery and show you where your mother is buried."

We reached the cemetery long before sunup. All of the graves were uncared for, and grass and weeds grew over them. Father pointed out my mother's grave. "Stay here and pray, if you wish," he said. "I have to go to work in the harvest."

I knelt by the grave and prayed. My tears came as I thought of my dear good mother and how she had struggled to keep us clothed and fed. I felt so lonely, and all day I couldn't shake off my depression. I went to the village priest and told him I would like to have a memorial service for my mother, and I made a donation to the church, which in Romanian money represented a rather large sum. Following the regular mass there was a beautiful mass in my mother's memory, but I was disturbed to note that Aunt Traiji was not there.

When we returned, I asked her, "Why didn't you come to the memorial service?"

"I have no shoes and I couldn't go barefooted," she replied. "The stones of the church floor are so rough and cold."

"Why didn't you tell me!" I exclaimed.

I gave her five dollars and, the following Wednesday, she went to the city market and bought herself the shoes she so much needed.

The people were all so poor. No one had any money. Because of the difficulty in sending money to Romania and of being sure it would reach the person for whom it was intended, I had brought money from American relatives to a number of people in Romania. I had it folded up into a handkerchief and pinned inside my corset.

I distributed the money that had been sent to those in Madarasul mare, and then went one day to my husband's village of Rusi to give money to those whose names were on my list. I asked them to come to a cousin's house to receive it. They came at the appointed time, and so did a great many other people. I began distributing the money; marking the names off the list as I gave each one the amount sent him.

One of my husband's cousins who had lived in America for a time called me into the kitchen.

"Be more careful," he cautioned. "These people are so starved for money, someone might hit you in the head for a hundred dollars or less."

After that, I was careful not to flash any money around.

I was in Romania for seven weeks and spent about half of that time in cities where I could get good coffee and eat anything I liked, but when I stayed with relatives, I was always hungry. All they had to offer was bacon and eggs, different kinds of soup, and chicken on Sunday. Very few of them had a cow and, since coffee was a luxury, they couldn't afford it so they just drank water. It was my pleasure to buy white bread, coffee, sugar, and liver sausage for them while I was there.

Just as we did years before, they took a lunch of raw bacon, bread and onions to the field. They have no way of building a fire while they are out at work and they wouldn't be allowed to anyway, because of the fire hazard.

One day, Julia went to the market to take some things to sell, and I stayed at home with her little girl and boy. Julia said for us to get bacon from the attic and fry bacon and eggs for our lunch.

When the time came, I got a big handful of straw and put it into the stove. Then I added wood, but I couldn't get the stove to draw, and the fire wouldn't burn. My little nephew said, "Mommy doesn't make the fire like you do. My mommy brings sunflower sticks first."

By that time, the kitchen was full of smoke and I was tired of trying to build a fire in that kind of a kitchen stove. I had lost my rabbit's foot for fire building. I said to the children through my smoke tears, "Do you know what we are going to have for lunch? Raw bacon!" And that is what we had.

Everything seemed so slow! My life had been keyed to the American pace, and I couldn't understand how they could be so unhurried. With the peasant women, work never ended, but a neighbor would come over and stand talking by the door for an hour. I remembered when I was a little girl, we had a neighbor who would talk and talk, but never sit down.

"No, I am in a great rush," she would say, and talk on and on.

When she would finally leave, my mother would say, "I could sew a wheat bag by hand while she talked!"

Accustomed as I had become to an automobile, walking seemed the slowest and most wearisome of all slow things. One day, my sister went to take dinner to her husband in the field. I asked her if I could go with her. She was barefooted and wore a babushka, which protected her from the sun. I was bareheaded and wore shoes.

It was very warm and my feet grew hot and tired. I removed my shoes, but my feet were so tender from long years of wearing shoes, that the clods of dirt hurt them. Finally, I had to sit down and put my shoes back on.

The beds made my back ache and the kerosene lamps seemed like lightening bugs after years of using electric lights. Julia didn't have fleas, but my cousin who came with them from America, complained bitterly of them.

There wasn't even a phonograph in the village. I understood there were a few radios in the large cities.

Far worse than the inconveniences in the home and in traveling was the inadequate food. The general health of the people was poor. Many suffered during the summer with some kind of fever. It seemed to me that almost everyone had it. The victim would begin to chill and shake, and even in warm July, would have to have heavy covers. No one seemed to go to a doctor for it. Many attributed the condition to hunger, more than anything else.

A childhood friend had recently lost her husband as the result of an operation for rupture. The man had spent a few years in America, but did not have the operation there.

My friend said sorrowfully, "If he had only had the operation while he was in America, I know the doctors could have saved him. But he came home and went to work in the field. His rupture got worse and worse, and they took him to the city and operated on him. He never came out from under the anesthesia."

A part of her bitter grief was that she could not bring him home to bury him.

Across the street from my sister lived an old friend of my mother's. She was very ill and I took her an apple I had brought from Aurora. She was so glad to see me and so pleased with the apple.

Her faith in God touches me, for she kissed me on the cheek and said, "It makes me happy to see you. I am dying and I know I will soon see your mother and talk to her. I will tell her that you came home on a visit and that I saw you. She will be so glad to hear."

She died about a week later. She had been on crutches for a year before her death, but had had no bed pan or slop jar to use. None of the peasant homes have indoor toilets, so whenever nature called, her family had to carry her out in the back yard. They did this to the day of her death.

I went to the wake the night before her burial. She may have been 60 or 65, but one who attains that age in Romania seems very old and, as a corpse, she looked hauntingly terrible. The following day, I attended her funeral.

The relatives carried the church banners during the funeral ceremony, and one of the men carrying a banner stood right back of the priest. This man was so tired and worn out from long hours of work in the harvest that every little bit he would go to sleep standing up and almost drop the heavy banner on the priest's head.

Finally, in the midst of the ceremony, the priest turned to him and said, "Either stay awake and hold the banner or give it to somebody else."

The funeral service for Mother's old friend was a sharp contrast to those held in Aurora, Illinois, where the expensive coffins were covered with beautiful flowers. A custom in Aurora which seemed strange to many Americans was that of having a picture made of the dead person in his coffin. The corpse would be so covered with flowers that only the head would be visible. All the friends and relatives who attended the funeral service would be photographed surrounding the coffin. I have many such pictures of relatives who are deceased. These pictures are now in the archives of the Aurora Historical Museum.

California, The Golden

After my return from Romania, our business prospered, until the big depression of the 1930's came along and the market crashed. Then we, like other business people, suffered. Many came to ask for credit and we helped as many as we possibly could. Some repaid US. Some did not. (We lost five or six thousand dollars we were never able to collect.)

On January 2, 1932, our oldest daughter, Emma, was married to Victor Trense. Emma was twenty years old when she married and pretty as a picture. We gave her the biggest wedding that had ever been in Aurora. The wedding feast was held at the Romanian hall and 1500 sat down to the table.

The ladies who prepared the dinner, began cooking on Wednesday, in order to be ready for Saturday night, when the wedding took place. Among other things, we had chicken soup, rolled cabbage, fried chicken, baked ham, beer and pop, and ice cream and cake. A firm we had patronized through the years made Emma a present of all the ice cream she needed to serve the guests.

Her wedding was in the American-Romanian tradition, with the Bride's Dance following the wedding feast.

Emma and Vic settled in a furnished apartment and she kept house until times became so bad that Vic was laid off work in the factory where he was employed. Then, one day, Emma announced that she wanted to come back to work in the store.

Ever since my trip to Romania, I had had a great desire to travel. Day after day, I looked out at the trains going by. Some bore large signs that read, "Go West," or "See America First."

So, now that our capable and experienced Emma wanted to return to the store, I suggested to my husband, "Let's you and George and me drive to Hot Springs, Arkansas, stay while, and then drive on to California. If we like it, maybe we can move to California. We can leave Mary and Florence with Emma and Vic, while we take the trip."

It wasn't hard to persuade my husband. We drove first to Hot Springs, and then followed the Southern route to California.

For me, the trip was like a lovely, lovely picture book: the rivers and the green grass, the sheep, and the horses, and the cattle, and the great fields of growing crops that were not yet ready for the harvest; the farm machinery, and the neat farm houses. How different it was from Romania, this great and wonderful America!

It seemed to me that everywhere we stopped in Texas, there would be a snakeskin stretched on the wall with a sign beneath it saying, "This rattlesnake was killed here. It has twenty-one (or twenty-three, or sixteen) rattles."

I began to feel sensitive on the subject of rattlesnakes and "watched my step," but on the whole trip, we never saw a rattlesnake crawling around with even one rattle.

At last, we found ourselves on the top of a mountain and I looked out and said, "Snow!"

"It couldn't be," said my husband. So, I got out of the car and gathered him a snowball.

We began to wind down and down around the mountain, and traveled great distances until we reached San Diego, about three o'clock in the afternoon.

We stopped to buy gas and my husband remarked, "We can make it to Los Angeles tonight."

"Not me!" I exclaimed. For years, when I was wrapped in wool and freezing in Illinois, I have read the papers and seen pictures of people dressed in white summer clothes, enjoying the sunshine of Tijuana. "I want to see "Tijuana."

So we drove to Chula Vista, California and stopped at a motel. The owner was a pleasant, happy-go-lucky fellow, and when he found we had never been in Old Mexico and wanted to see Tijuana, he took us across the border that night.

We listened to the Mexican music, watched the gambling games, and returned to the motel. The next day, we again went across the border and dined at the Patio Cafe in Agua Caliente.

We located our friends in Los Angeles and spent a couple of weeks with them. We looked at property and, before we left for Aurora, we bought a beautiful Spanish-type, four family flat on South Arapahoe Street.

We left most of our clothes with our friends and returned to Aurora, thinking we would come right back to Los Angeles, as soon as we could make arrangements with my daughter, Emma, and her husband to look after the store.

But, by the time we reached Aurora, I was sick and tired. Instead of returning at once to California, I went to the hospital for an operation.

When I was strong enough, we (my husband and I, and the unmarried children) drove back to California. Florence, who was fourteen, and, George, sixteen, did all the work of getting us settled in one of our flats.

So began out new life in Southern California.

Epilogue

Mom's continuing story covers her early life in Romania. Many short stories tell about the life and the customs of the days at the end of the Century (1900) and into the early 20th Century.

For the short stories in "Pigeon Hill" I have taken these stories from Mom's Memories, which deal with her leaving Romania to see her new life in America. The stories I have used include her marriage and the grocery store years on Pigeon Hill.

This book ends with the family moving to California.

Mom's stories continue with the years in Los Angeles, in Hollywood, return to Aurora, Illinois, and back to Hollywood.

Pop passed away in 1962 at age 72 (above Mom passed away....)

Mom passed away in 1994 at the age of 102.

Dear Mary left us in 2000 at the age of 86.

About the Author

George W. Trippon was born and raised in Aurora, Illinois on Pigeon Hill. He is a World War II Veteran, serving as a Corporal in the Quartermaster Corps of the U.S. Army from 1942–1944. In his youth, he was a dancer, educator, fashion designer and writer/publisher. He founded and operated the Trippon Fashion Center School of Dress Design in Hollywood, California for twenty-six years.

He starred in the TV series, *"Sew What's New,"* locally and on The Learning Channel from 1976 through 1992.

His books, "Becoming a Dress Designer" (1970–out of print) and *"Sewing Tricks and Treats"* and *"Let's Design, Cut, Sew and Fit with George W. Trippon"* (out of print) were enjoyed by fans across the country and in Canada.

The books *"Brady School Memories–1925 to 1930"* (1998) and *"Indian Creek"* (1999) precede this book and are the basis of this trilogy.

Mr. Trippon is now 85 years old and retired. His home is in Southern California.

Printed in the United States
811800003B